The Battle of Flodden Field

COLDSTREAM FROM THE SOUTH

The Battle of Flodden Field
The Defeat of the Scots by the English, 1513

Robert Jones

The Battle of Flodden Field
The Defeat of the Scots by the English, 1513
by Robert Jones

First published under the title
The Battle of Flodden Field

Leonaur is an imprint of Oakpast Ltd

Copyright in this form © 2011 Oakpast Ltd

ISBN: 978-0-85706-631-2 (hardcover)
ISBN: 978-0-85706-632-9 (softcover)

http://www.leonaur.com

Publisher's Notes

The opinions of the authors represent a view of events in which he was a participant related from his own perspective, as such the text is relevant as an historical document.

The views expressed in this book are not necessarily those of the publisher.

Contents

Preface	9
The Battle of Flodden Field	13
Notes	50

This Brief Account
Of the Battle of Flodden Field
Is Dedicated, by Permission, to
Louisa, Marchioness of Waterford,
Who, Since Her Residence at Ford Castle,
Has Taken a Deep Interest in
Everything Relating to that Memorable Event.

Preface

It has been my chief aim and desire, throughout the short account I have given of the Battle of Flodden, to carry the thoughts of my readers back to the time when the contending armies confronted each other, to the south of the village of Branxton. History and ballad have been the sources from which I have drawn most, if not all, of my principal events bearing on the battle; and in my notes I sincerely trust that I have elucidated many incidents which will enlighten those interested in the contest, and who may hereafter feel a wish to visit the field where so much heroism was displayed in former days by the ancient warriors of England and Scotland.

When occupied in writing my narrative of Flodden Field, however imperfect it may be considered, to me it was a source of much delight, for the short time engaged in the work; but more especially when contemplating that round about me once fought James IV. and Scotland's nobles, and the brave men under the command of the Earl of Surrey. In describing the position of both armies I have been most minute, knowing full well that the height of enjoyment to the tourist, when inspecting a field of battle, is to be able to fix his eye on the spot where each division stood before the fight commenced, and where the hottest struggle took place which decided the victory. This I have been in a great measure enabled to accomplish, from my long residence in Branxton, and thorough knowledge of the battle-ground; and also from different circumstances brought more immediately under my notice—such as the deposit of human bones found on the western end of the field, and the picking up of cannon-balls and coins, which undoubtedly bear an undeniable coincidence with the event.

Many of the marvellous accounts recorded by different historians who have written on the battle I have been careful in rejecting—such as the clouds of smoke which intervened between the two armies after the burning of the tents on Flodden Hill, and which is said to have intercepted the view of the English till they found themselves unexpectedly in close quarters with their foe—the great difficulties they had to contend with when climbing the precipitous rocks and banks to get at the Scotch—the want of provisions felt throughout the English camp for several days previous to the battle—the immense profusion of corn and wine found in the deserted camp belonging to the Scotch—the prodigious slaughter in King James's army, and the trifling loss of the English—the fabulous and absurd accounts respecting the murder of the King—and, lastly, the finding of his body on the battlefield.

All these extraordinary tales might be easily refuted were it deemed necessary to do so, but a few moments' reflection will cause us to cast them all aside, and dwell only on those events which must have taken place at the time of the battle, and a short period before the different armies met on the fatal field of Flodden. Scotland lost her King and the flower of her nobility, together with thousands of her heroic sons; and for years throughout her mountain-land of mist and rivers she sorrowed over the sad effects of the battle. Even at this time, the bare mention of Flodden causes the hardy sons of Scotland to mourn the loss of their country, on that day, "*when the flowers of the forest were a' wede away;*" and there is scarcely a schoolboy, from one end of the nation to the other, who has not read—

> *Still from the sire the son shall hear*
> *Of the stern strife, and carnage drear.*
> *Of Flodden's fatal field,*
> *Where shivered was fair Scotland's spear,*
> *And broken was her shield!*

England's loss amongst her common soldiers most not have been less than that of Scotland. Both nations suffered dreadfully on the field, and the joyous news of victory brought to Surrey the following morning caused him to give thanks to the Almighty that Flodden Field was won. Scotland, although she mourns the loss of her warriors in the battle, has not the least cause to sorrow for the valour and honour of her sons, for none could have fought with greater courage and more determined resolution than they did throughout the day. Rank after rank fell in the struggle, and their beloved King beheld his nobles and his men give up their lives cheerfully and heroically in his defence, and night alone put an end to the fury of the combatants.

The sketch I have given of the Field of Battle has been drawn, not, as it is now, divided into different farm-onsteads, but as it must have appeared when the battle was fought, with the exception of the vicarage-house in the centre. The hill on the left is where Flodden encampment stood, and the small eminence to the right of the church is what, in all probability, must have been known in those days as Piper's Hill, for there is no other elevated ground on the battle-field that could have been designated by that name.

The Bridge of Twizel is taken from an old engraving, and is an exact copy of what it was when Lord Thomas Howard passed the vanguard over, on his way to Flodden Field. Within the last thirty or forty years, (at time of first publication), the parapet has been taken down, and made straight at the top, which has destroyed the point in the centre represented in the etching; but in every other respect it is the same old original bridge. The fluted ribs in the arch have always been considered by the antiquary as possessing great strength and beauty, and well worth the trouble of a close inspection; so also is the rock beneath the castle, on account of St Helen's Well, and the petrifying property of the water which oozes from its fissures.

I may have indulged in some parts, when describing events and circumstances, in using language bordering on the heroic, but I beg my readers to bear in mind that my subject is *Flodden*

Field. By some I may be censured for inserting names and places, such as the fords on the banks of the Tweed, without having authority for doing so; but when history records that the army passed that river at Coldstream, there can be no danger of erring from the truth when the fords are particularised by name. And in some of my notes I may have digressed a little from my subject. Permit me, however, to say, that it has been my ambition throughout this little work to adhere as closely as possible to accuracy and truth—to do justice to King James, his nobles, and his men—and to describe the battle and events just as we may suppose they were when Flodden Field was fought.

Branxton Vicarage,
2nd August 1864.

TWIZEL BRIDGE

The Battle of Flodden Field

When recording an event which has taken place more than three hundred years ago, it is necessary that particular attention be paid to every historical fact, to every document, and every circumstance bearing on that event. Our information, as far as we are able to judge, must be gained from authentic sources; and before we can substantiate any occurrence of importance, as a fact to be relied on, we must give our proofs from history, or assign sufficient grounds, why we conclude that such and such things would have been done, and why they were done.

In my description of this great and important Border battle, which shook the kingdom of Scotland from one end to the other, and filled it with the deepest grief, I shall, in the first place, give a succinct account of the state of the feeling which predominated in the countries north and south of the Tweed; then describe the assembling of the two armies, their dress, and defensive weapons; and afterwards, notice any event or circumstance which more particularly points out the identical field on which the battle was so obstinately and so heroically fought.

A short time previous to these events, the two nations had petty grievances to complain of, which, although of minor importance, nevertheless stimulated each other to acts of reprisal, especially as neither would make concessions to the other. The Bartons in Scotland, and the Howards in England, had met and fought on sea: and the Borderers—those fierce, wild, and restless men, residing on the marches and the banks of the Tweed, belonging to both nations—had met in deadly combat time after time; sometimes few in number, headed by a daring and chosen chief; and at other times, but in more remote ages, under the command of the head of a clan—as a Douglas, a Home, or a Percy—when the strife for superiority, plunder, and victory, terminated in torrents of blood.

This hatred of each other had been unceasingly rankling and smouldering in the hearts of the men of England and Scotland for generations past, and it only required the aspiring touch of ambition to kindle this dormant spirit into a flame. From the days of the invasion under Edward I., whose barbarous cruelties had been felt from the banks of the Tweed to the Forth, the men of Scotland had justly and deliberately brooded over the wrongs inflicted upon them by that rapacious monarch. A Wallace and a Bruce had shewn what their countrymen could perform in daring feats of combat; and on the bloody field of Bannockburn—a battle which makes the heart of all true Scotchmen, even at this day, burn with heroic ardour—they had prostrated their most formidable foe, and tarnished England's glory.

From this time to the battle of Flodden, a deadly jealousy of each other's power had manifested itself at various times and in various ways. Scotland and France, for their own mutual benefit, were knit together by the closest bonds of friendship, and the intercourse between these two nations was of the most compact and durable nature, even continuing down to the unhappy days of the unfortunate, but ever-to-be-lamented, Mary Queen of Scotland.

The Border marches on both sides of the Tweed were occupied by men nursed in the cradle of contention and strife, and their chief, nay, we may almost say, their only delight, was in plunder and slaughter. No sooner had the sun gone down, and the shades of night appeared, than these bold fearless men dashed across the fords, pillaging and killing, robbing and destroying; and their most daring feats of personal valour and manly prowess resounded in tumultuous and boisterous joy at their wassail feasts, and in their homes, night after night, for the amusement and excitement of those who came to hear, to praise, and to laugh.

Many a resolute and hardy band of Scotchmen from Coldstream and its neighbourhood, allured by the love of enterprise and plunder, had crossed the Leet and Lennel fords for the south side of the Tweed; and many an Englishman, equally brave and resolute, had passed from the other side, under the protection of the castles of Norham and Wark, Etall and Ford, to commit the like depredations on the north side of the Tweed. Berwick, in those days of violence and blood, must have witnessed many a desperate encounter between foes whose animosity for each other was of so long and deadly a character; for whenever war was declared between the two nations, she was generally marked out as the bone of contention by each party, and the possession of the town and castle was always considered as the key to either kingdom.

No fortress on the Border was of greater importance than Berwick, and none underwent more changes from hostile attacks, even from the days of Alexander I. of Scotland, down to the troublesome times of Charles I. of England, when the town and castle were garrisoned by troops under, the immediate command of the Protector Cromwell. Such was the feeling and state of the countries of England and Scotland when King James IV. ascended the throne—a throne that was spotted at the very commencement of his reign with the blood of intestine war, which always haunted that monarch from the beginning of his sovereign authority to his untimely death on the fatal field of Flodden.

He had married Margaret, the eldest sister of Henry VIII., from which alliance we might conclude there would be peace between the two kingdoms; but, from the first day of his ascending the Scottish throne, his affection and interest, counsel and influence, turned to the old ally of his kingdom, the King of France (see **Note 1**). Henry, who had proclaimed war, and made every preparation for carrying it into effect, was on the eve of invading the French territory; his forces were collected together, and his ships were ready for their embarkation. He had, however, previous to his departure from England, appointed Thomas, Earl of Surrey, lieutenant-General of the northern counties, advising him to use all diligence and caution, and to neglect nothing that would tend to the welfare and security of his kingdom, for he had well-grounded suspicions that the King of Scotland was secretly preparing an army, either to assist the King of France, or to make inroads into his kingdom, with a view of invading it during his absence.

In the meantime James had done all he possibly could to persuade Henry to remain in England, and not interfere in the quarrel between Pope Julius and Louis XII. of France, but unfortunately all his entreaties were in vain; whereupon he instantly proclaimed war against England, well knowing that by so doing he should weaken the strength of Henry's army, by compelling him to send sufficient force to protect the northern parts of his kingdom. His plans were no sooner devised than they were put in execution; and for this purpose he ordered his fleet, consisting of 23 sail, 13 of which were large ships of war, with 3000 men on board, under the command of the Earl of Arran, a nobleman quite incompetent to execute such a trusty to sail for the coast of France, under the pretext that it was a present to Ann, Queen of that country. This armament, which had cost James such vast sums of money, failed in every purpose for which it was designed. This was the only fleet prepared for war by the King of Scotland, and we hear nothing worth noting respecting its future destination, with the exception that the Great Michael, the flag-ship of the Admiral, was purchased by the King of France after the death of James.

Scotland now sounded with the clang of the hammer from north to south, and from east to west; men were resolute and determined, full of heroic ardour for their king and country and for their own personal glory. Once more were their swords, spears, axes, and arrows sharpened and burnished for the deadly combat, after having lain for nearly a generation bygone in the dust and cobweb of their own mountain and lowland homes. The herald of war sent by their beloved King, had passed throughout the length and breadth of the land, summoning the men capable of bearing arms to meet him in the course of three weeks. This summons was obeyed by every man with alacrity, cheerfulness, and delight.

Bannockburn, with all its glory, and with all its results, was the watchword which passed from town to town, from mountain to mountain, and rested nightly on the compressed lips of all who had girded on the sword for the battle's strife. One hundred thousand men met together in this short space of time, fully equipped and accoutred, on the Borough Moor, near Edinburgh, with provisions for forty days, ready, at the word of their King, to march and to follow him to whatever part he chose to lead them. In this number, however, we must include the attendants and camp-followers, the usual train-concomitants of an army, and not consider them all as fighting men.—(See **Note 2.**)

The news of these warlike preparations stirred up the Border blood to feverish heat; men felt themselves carried away by restlessness and excitement; everyone was ready for revenge, and panted for conquest and for glory. Under these overpowering feelings, a band of Northumbrians, commanded by one of their chiefs, crossed the Tweed and entered Scotland, and, as a prelude to the war, commenced hostilities, by burning and pillaging and carrying off considerable spoil. This daring act of depredation so aggravated the Warder of the Marches, Alexander Lord Home, who had this part of the country under his more immediate protection and guardianship, that he hastily got together 3000 horsemen (Tytler mentions 8000), crossed the Tweed, laid the northern parts of Northumberland under contribution, burned several of the villages, and amassed much plunder, which many of this marauding party carried off in safety to their own country.

But as Lord Home and the rest of his men were returning in a careless manner loaded with spoil, through the woody country between Wooler and Milfield, they were suddenly surrounded by a large force of horse-archers and bowmen, under the command of Sir William Bulmer, who had concealed themselves amongst the trees and tall broom, through which the path lay that Home and his straggling horsemen were drowsily trotting their jaded steeds over.

This conflict was short, sharp, and deadly, but decisive. Four hundred were killed, many of them before they saw their enemy, or heard the twang of the bow that sent the messenger of death among them. More than two hundred were taken prisoners, amongst whom was George, the brother of Lord Home, who had accompanied him in this Border raid. He, however, and the rest of his men, fled with precipitation to the banks of the Tweed, and crossed the Leet ford, after leaving all their booty and a considerable number of horses in the hands of the victors. In these superstitious times, even trifling events were construed into acts of importance, and this failure on the part of the Scots at the commencement of the war, was considered by many as an omen of ill luck. This skirmish took place about a month before the Battle of Flodden, and was generally known by the name of "The ill rode."—(See **Note 3**.)

Be this as it may, there was no lack of resolution and manly prowess throughout Scotland. The flame of war had heroically kindled even in the bosom of the gentler sex; their fingers, like the Carthaginian ladies in the days of Hannibal, were occupied day and night in warlike preparations, and in embroidering pennons and flags, which their husbands, sons, and brothers swore to defend with their lives when in battle; and verily most truly and manfully did they fulfil their vows on the fatal field of Flodden. All was animation and excitement. From the Palace of Holyrood to the castle, there was the constant tramp of warriors cased in armour.

The wild music of their own mountain glens and Highland homes sounded in the dead of night, and the rattling of the horses' hoofs, together with the shrill ring of the trumpet, kept all in the highest state of inquisitiveness and curiosity. The messengers and heralds were passing to and fro, the streets were full of men and women; and whenever the King made his appearance amongst them, the enthusiastic clash of arms, and the exulting shout of defiance, flashed from eye to eye, passed from lip to lip, spread from throng to throng, till the echo from the rocky crags reverberated the prolonged martial sound.

Such was Scotland, and her romantic city, in the early part of August 1513. The King and the chief nobles of his kingdom held divers consultations respecting the proclamation of war with England. Many were against invading that kingdom, and the Queen used all her influence and entreaties to persuade him not to break peace with her brother. The arts of necromancy were called in to aid their cause, with the hope of diverting him from such a rash and hazardous enterprise. The superstition of the age was fraught with unnatural sights and wonders; the private chapel of Linlithgow was made the scene of ghostly apparitions (see **Note 4**) during the very time the King was on his knees at prayer; and unearthly ominous voices proclaimed in the dead of night, from the ancient Cross of Edinburgh, the names of many of the great men of Scotland who should fall on the day of battle.

Neither persuasion nor supernatural events had the least influence over the mind of James; he was fully bent on his warlike intentions, and no power on earth could divert him from them. His army stood now before him; men from all parts of his kingdom had obeyed his summons, and were ready to do his bidding (see **Note 5**). Never before or since had such a host of warriors assembled together in Scotland, and never were men more anxious to march across the borders of the Tweed. The only certain way of standing high in the King's favour was to embrace his views, to second his projects, and to give a willing and helping hand in furthering his design of invading England.

This passion for war was excited to the highest pitch by the fostering flattery of many of his nobles. Andrew Forman, Bishop of Moray, a man of mercenary character, who had been bought over by the gold of France, urged him with all his influence and persuasion to put in execution those ardent desires for war which had engrossed his constant thoughts for several months past. He represented by letter the cowardly act of delay, the base and dastard conduct of withholding from the strife, especially when his old ally was threatened with the danger of invasion from so powerful a foe as Henry, King of England. He painted in glowing colours the sure prospect of honour, glory, and victory, which was certain to crown his exertions the moment he crossed the Borders. Nothing was left undone or omitted that would stimulate him to begin and carry on the war; even the Queen of France had dubbed him her own true knight, and to this effect had sent him a ring from her own finger, of very great value, begging him by letter not to hesitate in his noble and manly purpose, "but to march, if it were only for her sake, three feet on English ground."

Everything being now in readiness, the camp on the Borough Moor was broken up, and orders were given that the army should march south for the banks of the Tweed. The drums and the trumpets sounded on every side and in every direction, and all was bustle and excitement. The whole inhabitants of Edinburgh and the neighbourhood for miles around had assembled together to witness the sight of 100,000 men marching to invade England. The Borough Moor was crowded with soldiers and horses, oxen and baggage-wagons, tents, pennons, and flags. The commanders of the different divisions and men-at-arms were clad in mail from head to foot, highly polished, and mounted on chargers of great power and mettle.

The Borderers rode horses of less strength and elegance, but of great speed and activity, and their armour was generally of a lighter description, more adapted for men accustomed to sadden forays, or for pursuing a routed enemy. The foot-soldiers were clad after the custom and manner of that part of Scotland from which they came. Those from the towns wore the steel cap and gorget, with a light coat-of-mail, fitting closely to the body, but in no way impeding either the arms or the legs. The men from the Lowlands wore the iron cap, fastened under the chin with scale-iron clasps, and their coats or jerkins were made of leather, or strong linen quilted with light scales of iron, overlapping each other, but perfectly flexible and strong, and proof against the arrow-point The Highlandmen retained the tartan and plaid, together with the blue bonnet and eagle's feather, much the same as those of the present Highland regiments, but of a coarser quality.

Their weapons were the bow and two-handed sword (see **Note 6**). Most of the foot-soldiers carried on their left arm the round shield or target, made of sheet-iron, plated tin, or wood covered with leather. Their weapons were the long spear, fifteen feet in length, fashioned after those used by the Grecian *phalanx*, and by the English at the Battle of Cressy; their swords were both long and short, either curved or straight, depending on whether they were worn by horse or foot soldiers; the former had also the short battleaxe, with edge and spear point, a most formidable weapon in close combat, made either to cut through the helmet or coat-of-mail, or to penetrate the head or body; and many carried the long Moorish pike, the bow, and sheaf of arrows.

Thus accoutred and equipped, the army set forward on its march for England. All were animated with hope, and acclamations and prayers for its success met it on every side, and in every town and village through which it passed. The heavy artiller, consisting of seventeen great guns—but, according to some historians, twenty-four—was drawn by oxen, and generally went in advance of the army, and the horse and foot followed in large divisions. In this manner the army passed through the country from Edinburgh to the banks of the Tweed.—(See **Note 7**.)

On Sunday, the 21st August 1513, the town of Coldstream was full of soldiers. The Lees' Haugh and the country round were covered with men and tents. Never before or since had such an armed host of Scotchmen met on the banks of the Tweed, and thousands on that night slept for the last time on Scottish ground. The sun had no sooner risen on Monday morning, the memorable 22nd August, than this vast assemblage of 100,000 men were all astir.

The King, in all the panoply of martial glory, passed from rank to rank, while his nobles, dressed in mail armour, headed their respective divisions, and the enthusiastic shouts of the men of all ranks were heard far and wide on the English side of the Tweed. The ford at the mouth of the Leet, and the one in those days on the haugh, a little to the west of the Dedda, and nearly opposite the mill at Cornhill, were crowded with men and horses, oxen, and baggage-wagons, crossing to the other side. The Borderers, under Lord Home, led the way, for they were considered as the vanguard of the army, being perfectly well acquainted with every inch of ground on both sides of the river, and no doubt but he and his men thirsted for revenge on account of their recent defeat on the plains of Milfield. He would eye with especial favour and martial joy, the different companies forming in lank and marching order, the moment they set their foot on English soil.

They were now in their enemy's country, and every face they met was that of a foe. The castles of Wark and Norham were immediately besieged, and soon fell into their hands (see **Note 8**). The latter was in those days garrisoned by men in the pay of Thomas Ruthal, Bishop of Durham, who, in his account of the Battle of Flodden, written only eleven days after the event, thus bemoans his loss to Cardinal Wolsey, then with King Henry before the walls of Terouenne:

> After right herty recommendations to reherse unto you the greate sorow and pensivenese that I have had and taken for the mysfortune of my castell at Norham, whiche, by the cruell tyrany of the King of Scots, was lately taken, and a greate part thereof rased and cast down.

He then goes on to say, but in a very strange and silly manner coupling St Cuthbert with the Almighty:

> But I thanke our Lorde God and my patrone Seint Cuthbert, who neir suffered anny iniurye, dispute, or displeasure doon to his Churche to passe onpunyshed, that greate, tyranows, and cruel dede is well requyted and revenged.

For on the ix. day of this instante monethe of September, after a muclouse greate conflicte and terrible bataill, the King of Scots, with the greatest parte of the lords and nobles of his reame, wer in playne bataill vanquyshed, outhrown, and slayn.

The castle of Norham was taken possession of on Monday the 29th, one week after crossing the fords near Coldstream. Considerable plunder was found within the walls, all of which was carried away by the Scotch.

Etall Castle was next attacked, and soon fell into their hands; but before Ford Castle (see **Note 9**), which was then occupied by Lady Heron, there was more difficulty to contend with. Stipulations had been made by that lady under peculiar arrangements, that her castle should not be thrown down (see **Note 10**). These were agreed to by James under certain conditions, but whether fulfilled or not on Lady Heron's part, history is scant on the subject; for it is very well known that the assault took place, and considerable damage was done to the castle (see **Note 11**). This lady has been accused of playing a deceitful part towards the King; for at that time, though she in all appearance seemed friendly to his cause, she was carrying on a secret correspondence with the Earl of Surrey, and giving him a full account of the Scottish army, the castles they had assaulted and taken, the number and condition of the men, and the position of their camp on Flodden Hill.—(See **Note 12**.)

England in the meantime had not been dormant; she had her emissaries and her spies in all parts, especially along the Borders. From Berwick to Carlisle, the Border-prickers, on their fleet and wiry steeds, were to be heard of, and many passed over stealthily on foot, to hear and see what Scotland was doing. Even the movements in the Palace of Holyrood and on the Borough Moor were not concealed from her; and although the mode of travelling in those days was not so quick as with us, yet did intelligence of the army crossing the Tweed reach the Earl of Surrey in a very short time, notwithstanding he was then more than two hundred miles from Coldstream. News from the north of

England was greedily sought after by men in the south, and the rumours of war were the engrossing topics, from the peasant to the prince.—(See **Note 13**.)

In the latter end of July, Surrey marched through the streets of London, with a few hundreds of his retainers, on his way to Yorkshire. The Castle of Pontefract was made the rendezvous, where many of the warriors were to meet Here plans were formed, and orders given, for summoning the horse and foot soldiers to make all possible speed to meet him in Newcastle. In this town he was joined by Lord Dacre, who commanded the horse, Sir William Bulmer, Sir Marmaduke Constable, and many others belonging to the northern counties. Cheshire, Lancashire, Westmoreland, and Cumberland sent their thousands from the west; and Yorkshire, Durham, and Northumberland from the east (see **Note 14**).

At this critical time Lord Thomas Howard, High Admiral of England, landed at the mouth of the Tyne, with 5000 soldiers, sent from the army in France by the King, to assist in protecting his kingdom. Before Surrey left Durham, the celebrated banner dedicated to St Cuthbert was delivered to him by Bishop Ruthal, whose childish superstition of its marvellous power is ridiculously mentioned in the letter from which I have already quoted. England was agitated throughout her northern counties; the war-feeling had kindled in the breast of her warriors, and they had buckled on their armour, and put themselves in readiness for the battle fray. The Queen herself had become infected with the chivalrous contagion. She and her ladies, like those in Scotland, were closely employed in making flags and colours; and in one of her letters to Cardinal Wolsey she expressed herself thus:

> I am horribly busy in making standards, banners, and badges.—(See **Note 15**.)

Men from the east, west, and south of England came pouring on in quick succession. Durham and Newcastle were thronged with horse and foot soldiers. Day and night brought fresh supplies. No sooner had thousands marched on for the north, than thousands took up their places from the south. The watchword that the King of Scotland had invaded England, and was throwing down castle after castle, spread with astonishing rapidity from town to town, and every tongue resounded with the depredations committed by the Scottish army. Surrey had ordered all the men capable of bearing arms to hurry on for Alnwick, a town whose inhabitants knew well the strife of Border war, even from the days of Malcolm III. , King of Scotland, whose blood was treacherously spilt before her gates, to the hour when Surrey's forces assembled within her walls, on their march for Flodden Field.

By the 5th September their tents were pitched at Bolton, a small hamlet about five miles west of Alnwick, and north of the River Aln. Here they were joined by the Borderers and the men of Northumberland, under their different commanders, all animated with the greatest zeal of doing battle with their foes. They were clad much in the same manner as the Scotch. The leaders and the men-at-arms rode strong powerful horses, and they were covered from head to foot in burnished mail-armour. The warriors in those days never considered themselves equipped for battle unless they were cased in steel or iron. The struggle for victory was generally hand-to-hand, especially after they had discharged their arrows, so that the shock of battle was more terrible when each man singled out his foe, and was determined to conquer or to die, than it even now is, under all the improvement of the destructive implements of war. A few hours' combat sufficed to cover the field with the dead and dying. The arrow and spear-points soon did their fatal work; and the bill, the battle-axe, and the sword, wielded in the hands of the combatants, quickly laid their thousands in the dust.

The two armies were now drawing nearer and nearer to each other, the day of battle was close at hand, a few hours wafted intelligence from camp to camp, and all were preparing for the encounter. Surrey had challenged the King to meet him on Friday, the 9th September, and James had accepted the challenge, telling him "that had he been in Edinburgh, he would gladly have hastened to obey the summons." At this time the King was strongly encamped on the eastern end of Flodden Hill, a position that commanded a view of the country to the north and east, and looked directly across that part of Northumberland over which he expected the English army to march. The Till, a deep, slow, sluggish river, lay on the north side, and extended, with its tributaries, from the neighbourhood of Wooler to the Tweed, by Twizel Bridge; consequently, he neither expected nor dreaded an enemy from that quarter.

Surrey, on the afternoon of Tuesday the 6th, removed his army from the field at Bolton to Wooler Haugh, where he encamped till the morning of the 8th. After having tried different plans to induce James to meet him on Milfield Plain (see **Note 16**), but without success, he gave orders for his men to break up their encampment, and to march in the direction of Doddington, through which village the English army passed on their way to Barmoor Wood, where they encamped for the night.—(**See Note 17.**)

This sudden movement of Surrey caused James to turn his watchful eye towards Scotland. All was surmise and conjecture throughout the camp on Flodden Hill, and no one could assign a satisfactory reason why he marched on the north side of the Till, in a direct line for the banks of the Tweed. But no sooner had the fatal day arrived, when the two armies, in accordance with the challenge given and accepted, were to meet, than Surrey's host was on the move, and the mystery was revealed. Orders were given that the artillery and heavy baggage were to pass over the bridge at Twizel, and the vanguard under Lord Thomas Howard was to march in the same direction (see **Note 18**). The passing of the English army over the bridge at Twizel, is thus graphically drawn by Scott in his poem of *Marmion*:—

From Flodden ridge
The Scots beheld the English host
Leave Barmoor Wood, their evening post,
And heedful watched them as they crossed

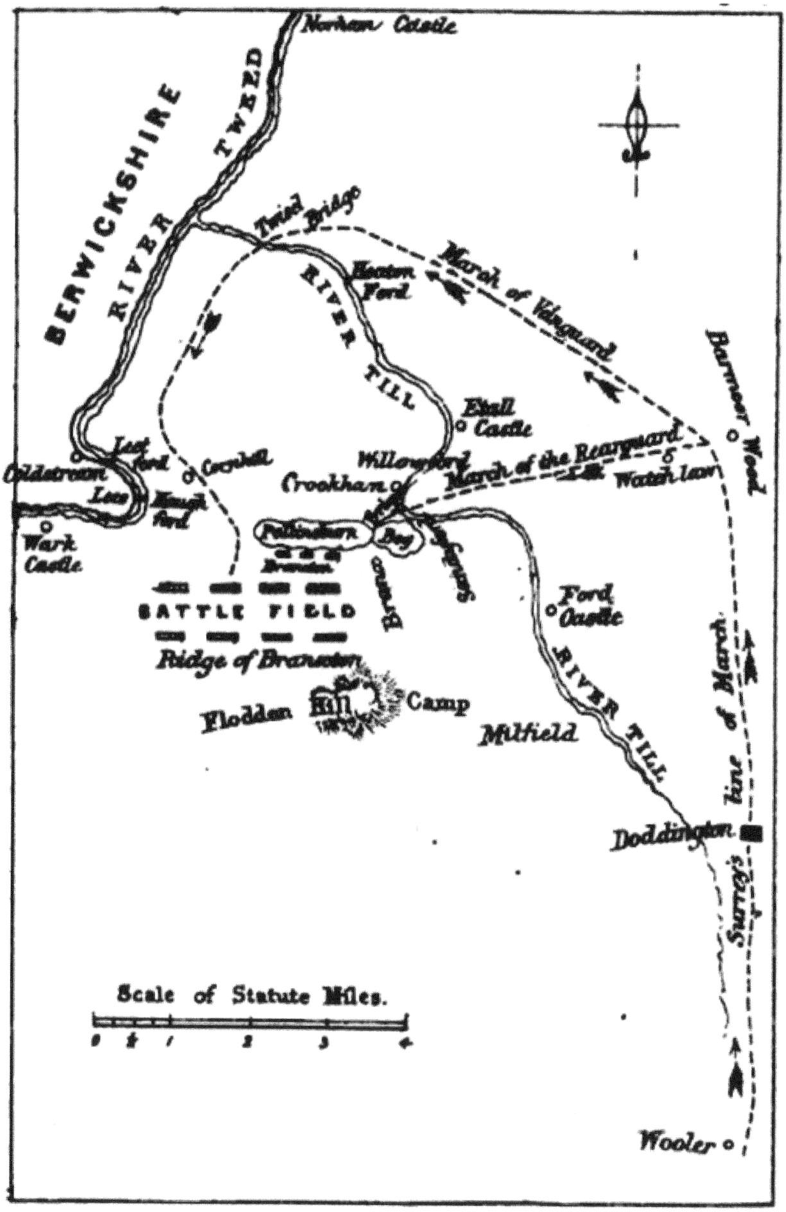

Norham Castle
BERWICKSHIRE
RIVER TWEED
Twisel Bridge
Heaton Ford
RIVER TILL
March of Vanguard
Barmoor Wood
Etall Castle
Willowford
March of the Rearguard
Watch law
Crookham
Coldstream
Lees Ford
Cornhill
Lees Haugh Ford
Wark Castle
Pallinsburn
Bog
Branxton
Sandyford
BATTLE FIELD
Ridge of Branxton
Flodden Hill Camp
Milfield
Ford Castle
RIVER TILL
Doddington
Surrey's line of March
Wooler
Scale of Statute Miles.
0 ½ 1 2 3 4

The Till by Twizel Bridge.
High sight it is, and haughty, while
They dive into the deep defile;
Beneath the caverned cliff they fall.
Beneath the castle's airy wall.
By rock, by oak, by hawthorn-tree.
Troop after troop are disappearing;
Troop after troop their banners rearing,
Upon the eastern bank you see.
Still pouring down the rocky den.
Where flows the sullen Till,
And rising from the dim-wood glen.
Standards on standards, men on men,
In slow succession still.
And, sweeping o'er the Gothic arch.
And pressing on, in ceaseless march.
To gain the opposing hill.

From Barmoor Wood to Twizel Bridge, and to the banks of the Till by Crookham, all was commotion and bustle, for the different divisions were marching to the various points assigned them by their commanders. The fords across that river, from the castle at Ford to its confluence with the Tweed, were well known to many in the English army. The Bastard Heron, who was born and brought up in the country—a daring Border trooper, who did good service in the battlefield, and who had very recently joined Surrey—together with Sir William Bulmer and others perfectly acquainted with all the natural difficulties of the river, were present to give counsel on that eventful day; and before noon thousands were across the Till, forming in the different companies in which they were to march to Flodden.— (See **Note 19**.)

We may well suppose that so many soldiers hastening for the battlefield would be the engrossing news of the day. Surrey's movements would reach Berwick and Coldstream long before Lord Thomas Howard had passed all his men, artillery, and heavy baggage over Twizel Bridge. The encampment at Flodden would be closely watched by all the Borderers, and every eminence in the neighbourhood of Coldstream would be covered with spectators. Many a gallant Scotchman would cross the Tweed at the mouth of the Leet (see **Note 20**), either with a determination of mingling in the fight, or with the intention of plundering his enemy should he be worsted in the battle. The field above the monument leading to the bridge, called the "Gallows Knowe," would be crowded with men and women. The whole town of Coldstream would be there, viewing the Scotch army taking up its position on the ridge of Branxton Hill; and at that distance many would be able to see the King's flag "fluttering in the breeze."

At the time the English army encamped at Barmoor Wood there were two celebrated fords across the Till, lying between the castles of Ford and Etall; one called the Willow ford, a little to the north of the village of Crookham, in the direction of Etall; the other to the east of Crookham, called Sandyford. The Heaton ford is not so much as mentioned by any ancient writer of this battle; nor can I understand how, at this day, it should be pointed out as the ford over which part of the English army passed when marching for the battlefield. It is surrounded on the north side with precipitous banks, not at all calculated for a multitude of men and horses clothed in armour to cross over; indeed, I am fully persuaded that this was not the ford over which the Earl of Surrey and the rearguard passed on their march for the field of battle.

From Watchlaw, an eminence east of the Etall, and from Barmoor Wood, where they encamped for the night, almost a direct line may be drawn, leading to a haugh or tongue of land bounding the Till below Crookham. The two fords alluded to are placed here, and one retains to this day, (as at time of first publication), the very name mentioned by Hall, who wrote an account of the battle in 1548, or thirty-five years after it had taken place, as "the little brook called Sandyford," over which the English passed; and the old ballad, which is supposed to have been written not later than Queen Elizabeth's time, also mentions this ford (*vide* Map):

> *And never flee while life did last,*
> *But rather die by dint of sword;*
> *Thus over plains and hills they passed,*
> *Until they came to Sandyford.*

With these strong evidences before me, I do not hesitate in affirming, that this is the very ford through which Surrey and the rearguard dashed, although mentioned in such a trifling manner as "a brook of breadth a tailor's yard." The small stream of Pallinsburn (see **Note 21**) empties itself into the Till at this place, and is known by the same name, which certainly might be stepped over, being not more than three or four feet in breadth.

Before the army commenced its march from Barmoor Wood, no doubt the village of Branxton would be mentioned as the place of rendezvous, at which both the vanguard and the rearguard should meet (see **Note 22**). At the time of the battle, and for more than two centuries after, a low piece of ground lying to the north of the parish of Branxton, through which the small stream of Pallinsburn runs, was covered with water to the extent of more than a mile and a half in length, and in many parts more than two hundred and fifty yards across. In the centre of this bog, or moat of water, and opposite the road leading to Mardon, there was an ancient bridge, called by the old people "Branx Brig." This bridge, according to the tradition of the oldest inhabitants whose ancestors for generations resided in Branxton and the neighbourhood, was always pointed out as the bridge over which the English passed on their way to the battle. The foundations of this bridge were to be seen thirty or forty years ago; and, indeed, some of the stones still remain, but in making proper levels through the bog the greater part has been moved away.

The rearguard, after having passed Sandyford, would inarch westward for the village of Branxton; one part might pass to the south of Pallinsburn bog, and the other through the centre over "Branx Brig," both close in sight of each other, and take up their position south and east of the village. The vanguard, under Lord Thomas Howard, would march, after passing over Twizel Bridge, on the beaten road by way of Cornhill, then turn for the Bareless toll, on the road that formerly led for Branxton, and take up its position to the west of the church and village, both of which in those days were considerably larger than at present.

These two columns, although a few miles apart, would be in constant communication with each other. The Borderers, on their fleet steeds, would be galloping to and from each division; orders would be given, received, and cheerfully obeyed, by men who were expecting every minute to be engaged in deadly combat with their enemy. All eyes would be turned towards the Scotch army, posted in battle array on the hill before them, and every man would hasten to take up the place assigned him on the battlefield by his commander.

The vanguard under Lord Thomas Howard, assisted by his brother, Sir Edmond Howard, and Sir Marmaduke Constable, formed in position to the south-west of the church, In the fields leading to Moneylaws; behind these three divisions were placed the baggage-wagons, as a protection to their rear; and amongst these soldiers was the standard-bearer. Sir John Forster, belonging to the bishopric of Durham, who carried aloft the banner of St Cuthbert. The Earl of Surrey, who commanded the rearguard, was placed near the vicarage-house, assisted by Sir Philip Tilney, Henry Lord Scrope of Bolton, and others of the nobility of the northern counties; and on his right and left by Lord Dacre, with 2000 horse drawn up in his rear, immediately in and around the village, extending a little to the west of the church, and near the centre of the whole English line, in readiness to give assistance wherever he and his men might be required.

With Dacre was the Bastard Heron, who also commanded a large troop of horse, than whom none was more formidable on the field, and none more willing for the battle-encounter. On his left, eastward, he was ably supported by a numerous division of horse and foot soldiers, under the command of Sir Edward Stanley, assisted by Sir William Molyneux and Sir Henry Kick-

A VIEW OF THE BATTLE GROUND OF FLODDEN FIELD

ley, from the county of Cheshire, placed on the fields south-east of the village leading to Mardon.

The English forces, now drawn up in six divisions, extending from the east to the west of the village, would cover considerably more than a mile and a half in length; but, from the narrow position of the ground, nearly all in a line. The westward division under Lord Thomas Howard, would be hid from the rest of the English forces on account of an elevation of ground a few hundred yards from the church, supposed to be the "Piper's Hill" alluded to in history, around which the most deadly conflict took place, and where it is supposed the King fell.—(See **Note 23**.)

Opposite this formidable force stood the Scottish army on the ridge of Branxton Hill, waiting anxiously the order for commencing the dreadful onslaught. To the extreme left, on the sloping part of the hill, looking towards Wark Castle, Home Castle, and Coldstream, were drawn up the wild and undisciplined Highlanders and stout Borderers under Huntly and Lord Home; to the right of these forces, looking north, those troops under Crawford and Montrose; a little farther east the chivalric King, with many of his nobles, both in chinch and state, who comprised the best and bravest blood of Scotland; on his right, on the gentle slope of the eastern end of Branxton ridge, was the right wing under Lennox and Argyle; and the reserve under Bothwell, a little to the south-east of the King's troops.

In this position stood the contending armies opposite each other before the battle began—one elevated considerably above his opponent, and commanding one of the most splendid views in the country, looking over the greater part of Berwickshire and Roxburghshire, and even extending beyond the hilly country of Selkirkshire,

Where not a mountain rears its head unsung.

With this beautiful landscape before them to the far west and north-west, and the English army below them steadily forming in position, and preparing for the battle that was on the eve of commencement, thousands of the bravest men of Scotland, together with their beloved King, viewed for the last time the country that gave them birth, and which was shortly to weep and mourn over the death of so many of her great and heroic sons.

Dr Leyden, in a note to his Ode on Flodden Field, mentions that, on the evening previous to the battle, the Earl of Caithness, a young nobleman who had incurred King James's displeasure for revenging an ancient feud, came to the encampment on Flodden Hill with three hundred young warriors, all dressed in green, and submitted to the King's mercy. James was so pleased with this mark of submission, that he granted to him and his followers an immunity for past offences. The parchment on which this immunity was inscribed is said to be still preserved in the archives of the Earls of Caithness, and is marked with the drumstrings—having been cut from the head of a drum, no other parchment being at hand. The Earl and his gallant followers perished to a man the next day on the fatal field of Flodden, ever since which time it has been considered unlucky in Caithness to wear green, or to cross the Ord on a Monday, the day of the week on which he set out to join the King.—(See **Note 24**.)

The positions of the English forces were drawn up to face the different divisions of the Scotch army, where they had been for several hours patiently waiting the approach of Surrey; for no sooner was it made known to James that the English were crossing the Till, than he moved from his encampment on Flodden Hill, and took possession of the ridge of Branxton Hill, which gave him a fall view of the country for several miles, over which the van-guard was marching, after having crossed the bridge of Twizel. He is blamed by several historians for abandoning his camp, where he was so strongly fortified; but anyone who has examined the position of the ground, and taken into consideration the flank movement of Surrey, who was then marching between him and Scotland, and by this masterly manoeuvre exposing the rear of his camp, and cutting him off from his own country, must admit that the King displayed no mean talent in

ARRANGEMENT OF TROOPS BEFORE THE BATTLE.

Lennox & Argyle.

Bothwell.

The King.

Crawford & Montrose. Errolle & Home.

Lord Tho.ˢ Howard &
Sir Ed. Howard.

Branxton Ridge, or Hill

Piper's Hill

Surry.

Dacre Horse.

Horse.

Stanley

Village of Branxton.

generalship when he selected such an advantageous and commanding position as that of Branxton Hill.—(See **Note 25**).

The armies being now put in battle array, confronting each other, stood thus upon the field: Lord Thomas Howard, with the van-guard, was opposite Huntly and Home, Crawford and Montrose; the Earl of Surrey had chosen the ground opposite the King, where the royal standard was flying, and which positions were the centres of each army; Sir Edward Stanley, who commanded the left wing of the rearguard, was opposite Lennox and Argyle (see **Note 26**). The cannons were placed in front along the two lines, at proper intervals between each division; and from the cannon-balls picked up at various times on the field, we may almost conclude, from the position in which they were generally found, that the greater number of shot fired by the Scotch were leaden balls, and by the English iron,—(See **Note 27**.)

It was now drawing near to four o'clock, and the sun was descending in the western sky; the clouds of night were about to cover the earth, yet was there time enough for thousands of the brave men who were standing gazing at each other, in the full vigour of manhood and health, to be laid in the dust, when, lo! men were seen galloping along the brow of the hill, and on the plain below, from rank to rank, and the trumpets sounded for the charge. All were in readiness and eager for the battle; the voices of the different commanders were distinctly heard, the clash of armour grated for a moment harshly on the ear, when in the next all was deadened by the roar of the guns and the shouts of men engaged in deadly strife.

> *Then ordnance great anon out brast*
> *On either side with thundering thumps.*
> *And roaring guns, with fire fast,*
> *Then levelled out great leaden lumps.*
>
> Old Ballad.

The thunder of the cannon soon ceased on both sides, without doing any serious injury to either; a few shots from each party sufficed, neither of which could be considered very proficient in the art of gunnery. The ground was uneven, and from the elevation of the guns on the English side, and the depression on the Scotch, the shot fell either short of the object aimed at, or passed considerably over the heads of the men, for many balls have been found north and south of the field of battle, and also along the side of the hill where the Scotch were stationed. Such fighting was too slow and desultory in its effects to satisfy either the one or the other; both sought closer quarters, and the struggle throughout was maintained from hand to hand. It is admitted by all who have written an account of the battle, that the vanguard, under Lord Thomas Howard, was first attacked.

His brother, Sir Edmond Howard, being in the extreme west of that division, on the fields leading to Moneylaws, was suddenly confronted by the Borderers under Lord Home (see **Note 28**), and the Highlanders under Gordon, Earl of Huntly. They had descended from the hill with a shout and slogan-cry to meet the men under Bryan Tunstall, who were ascending the lower acclivity, and they were immediately engaged in close combat with their enemy. Nothing could withstand the bold impetuosity of this attack The English were driven from their ground several times, but, cheered on by their commanders, returned again and again to the charge. The ground in a very short time was literally strewed with the dead and dying. Men fought with stubbornness and resolution—the Highlanders with their bows and two-handed swords (see **Note 29**), and the Borderers with their long spears.

Three times was Sir Edmond Howard felled to the ground, Tunstall lay dead among the slain, the men began to waver, and at last they fled, leaving Home and Huntly masters of this part of the field after long and continued fighting. Just at this critical and important period, Lord Dacre and the Bastard Heron, who was slightly wounded, came to the rescue with a large body of horse which had already been engaged in other parts of the field, and effectually stopped the victorious career of the left wing of the Scottish army. The sword and the spear came again in close contact, and men fell fast under the point and thrust of both. Several of Lord Home's friends were killed at this charge (see **Note 30**); but he managed to maintain his ground, and kept possession of it throughout the day and night, guarding the numerous prisoners taken on the field, amongst whom was Sir Philip Dacre, brother of the commander of the horse.

No sooner had Lord Home and Huntly commenced the battle than the troops under Crawford and Montrose moved down the slope of the hill. The Admiral now saw the critical position in which he stood, and, knowing full well the advantage the Scotch had in seeing the length and breadth of the field, sent hastily to his father, the Earl of Surrey, imploring him to engage the troops before him. The rising ground spoken of as "Piper's Hill" lay between the van and the rearguard, so that nothing, as I have previously mentioned, that was going on with the one division could possibly be seen by the other. Whereupon Lord Thomas Howard (see **Note 31**), to shew his anxiety for the fate of the day, took from his breast his *Agnus Dei*, and sent it by a messenger to his father, as a pledge of his earnest entreaties to begin with the centre, or to come to his assistance. In the meantime the King, observing the conflict on his left, and that the troops under Crawford and Montrose, as well as those under Huntly and Home, were hotly engaged, gave orders that all around him should march down the side of the hill and mingle in the fight (see **Note 32**).

His bodyguard was principally composed of the Scotch nobility—men of war and of indomitable energy and courage, whose very life was the breath of the battlefield, their highest glory "the raptures of the strife," and on the gory field of Flodden they sealed their loyal devotion to their King with the last drop of their blood. His heroic bravery would not allow him to filch a victory from his enemy; and sooner than it should be said that he availed himself of an unfair advantage, he rashly gave up his commanding position on the brow of the hill, and plunged down into the thickest of the battle. Had he but calmly and patiently waited for the English to attack him on the ground he occupied, which only could have been done after breathless exertion and great slaughter, in the face of men resting comparatively at ease, the struggle for victory might have terminated in the total defeat of Surrey's troops. The reserve under Bothwell followed close in the rear of the King, and at this moment thousands throughout both armies steadily moved in the direction of Piper's Hill, where the battle was continued with dreadful carnage during the closing moments of that fearful and bloody day.

Sir Edward Stanley, in the eastern division, had been fiercely engaged with the right wing of the Scotch under Lennox and Argyle; but the conflict here was not of long duration, although tracked with streams of blood. The English archers, composed principally of men from Cheshire and Lancashire, did terrible execution on the close ranks of the Highlanders and Islesmen; they fell thick on all sides, and the repeated showers of the unerring long-shaft arrows broke their solid masses, and put them in confusion. Lennox and Argyle, together with many experienced French officers in this division, did all they could, by entreaties and menaces, to cause the troops to stand firm in their ranks on the ground they then occupied, but without effect; for they instantly rushed down the hill and engaged their foes (who were rapidly ascending to meet them) in close combat.

The English billmen at the first onset staggered under the charge, and were obliged to give way—the onslaught was so fierce and sudden that it bore down all opposition; but this short success on the part of the clansmen at last gave way, and the undisciplined Highlanders were assailed in front and flank. The struggle for victory was dreadful; the English billmen laid hundreds dead at their feet, and Lennox and Argyle, with many of the chiefs of the clans, fell bravely fighting at the head of their men.—(See **Note 33**.)

The left wing of the English was completely victorious; their enemies were routed and driven from the field, and scattered in all directions; so much so, that they never again rallied. Stanley had now cut his way through all opposition to the top of the hill, from whence he could see the dreadful struggle that was going on in the centre and right wing; and he fall well knew, from the masses of men crowding together around the southern base of Piper's Hill—from the waving of flags and pennons, from the shrieks of the dying, and from the clash of arms—that the battle was raging in all its fury to the west below him. He hesitated not a moment; orders were given to his men, flushed and elated with success, to march in the direction of the combatants; and, passing hastily over the ground where the royal standard had fluttered before the battle had commenced, he rushed down with his forces in the rear of the King, where all now were contending and struggling for life and for victory.

By this strategic manoeuvre the fate of the day was completely changed. The Cheshire and Lancashire men, numbering after their struggle nearly ten thousand, came to the rescue of Surrey and the Admiral at that opportune moment, when the Scotch were upon the eve of victory. Home was cutting up with fearful havoc the extreme right of the English, and driving them in confusion eastward on the field. The King and Bothwell, with the troops under the command of Crawford and Montrose, were closely engaged with Surrey and the Lord Admiral, when Stanley came pouring on in quick advance with his conquering host to the encounter (see **Note 34**). This force would be seen by the different combatants descending with hurried steps the slope of the hill above them; and while to the Scotch it told the harrowing tale that the troops under Lennox and Argyle had been defeated and overthrown, it bespoke to the English that powerful succour was at hand in the hour of need, and they had only to fight on till Stanley and his men closed on the rear of James and Bothwell.

The bill and the bow, wielded in the hands of the victors, told terribly on the Scottish rear, which was instantly compelled to face about and contend with men who had just arrived from the slaughter of their right wing. The preponderating numbers now on the English side began to thicken darkly around them, and every step this crushing force advanced crowded in closer space the troops under the King and his nobles (see **Note 35**). The arrow, shot even at random, found a quiver of flesh to rest in, for the Scotch who stood on the gently elevated ground on the south side of Piper's Hill, could be picked off with unerring and deadly certainty. To Stanley and his stalwart yeomen, England is indebted for the victory on Flodden Field; for had he hesitated and remained a spectator of the contest below him only for a short time, the day, which was closing fast, would have set its sun on a battle equally as bloody and fatal to the English as Bannockburn had been.

Crawford and Montrose had been early engaged with the numerous forces under the Lord Admiral The Scotch troops under these two commanders, chiefly composed of men from the interior counties of Scotland, together with several lords and knights, were fiercely attacked by the English forces. The contest raged with dire effect on both sides, but at last the valour and discipline of the men under the Admiral prevailed, and Crawford and Montrose were counted among the slain.—(See **Note 36**.)

The battle had now continued with unabated fury for more than three hours, the left wing belonging to both armies had been victorious, thousands lay dead and dying on the field; but the fate of the day was far from being decided. The King, with his nobles, spiritual and temporal, had at the first dismounted from their horses, and marched on foot with their divisions down the hill into the thickest of the fight. By this noble act of devotion he had shewn to the men around him that he was determined to conquer or to die (see **Note 37**). All were animated with the like enthusiasm, and all were prepared to fall in defence of their King and country.

Never were more noble devotedness and heroism displayed, either in ancient or modem times, than was that day exhibited on the battlefield by the King, his nobles, and his men. At last the Scotch were completely surrounded. The Earl of Surrey was in front and on their right flank. Lord Thomas Howard on their left, and Sir Edward Stanley on their rear. Thus hemmed in on all sides, but not in despair, or in the least daunted or discouraged at their perilous and desperate position, they fought and fell, and victory ofttimes trembled in the scale. The billmen plied their ghastly strokes, cutting through the helmet and plaited armour, and the long spear did its fatal work. Men were falling fast on both sides; the shout and slogan-cry that urge to the fight, that animate and strengthen the heart and hand of the warrior on the day of battle, were heroically and defiantly uttered anon and anon by both combatants; there was no shrinking back, no standing still; every hand was lifted up to strike, or bent to give the piercing thrust

Wherever the King moved there was death; the struggle for victory was most terrific, and so long as James was able to command and shew himself in the ranks of his men, the day was neither lost nor won. The endurance and intrepidity which had signalised him throughout the battle never forsook him nor seemed to flag, and he had the happy method of inspiring all about him with the same heroic ardour. He and his nobles fought hand to hand with the English billmen, and many of them were cut down, and perished around the King. Here the throng of the battle's strife was the hottest. Nothing could surpass the resolute bravery of the combatants, for it was about his person that the serried ranks so nobly fought and fell. Many were the feats of individual heroism performed by either combatant At last the ground became sodden with blood, and woe to that man who slipped his foot in the clotted gore beneath him!—(See **Note 38.**)

On this spot the battle raged with the most destructive fury. There was no chance of recovering a false step once made, for the pressure of the masses on both sides was so greats and the contest so deadly urgent, that many were trampled to death by the contending wave that rolled so furiously above them. Inch after inch was only won by the death of hundreds, and the advantage which was so dearly bought one moment was lost in the next. Every one throughout the battle fought as if he felt that the victory of that day depended solely on his own arm and

persevering steady conduct on the field. There
mêlée in the encounter, with the exception of t
Lennox and Argyle; firmness and determinatic
on the countenance of each warrior, and the co
deadly effect in a series of single combats. All tha
was done on that fatal day. Scotland's glory; and
were neither tarnished nor sullied by the comb
recorded in the page of history that the northern spear was even
more fatal than the English axe or bill.

Fortune; which had soared and lingered so long over the heads of both armies, now began to droop; the King himself was wounded by an arrow, and soon after cut down by an English billman (see **Note 39**). In the midst of the blood and carnage that fringed the circle around him, he scorned to survive the death of so many of his devoted and gallant followers, and with them he boldly perilled the dangers of the fight. He hesitated not to engage in deadly combat his inveterate foe, whether of high or low degree.

Whoever stood confronting each other immediately strove for victory; and it was not till repeated wounds of ghastly depth, and loss of blood, that he fell on the field, where he had displayed the greatest courage and energy, and which will ever be held sacred by all true patriots wherever history records the death of James IV. of Scotland. He fell covered with honour amongst the slain, of his nobles, who throughout the battle had never shrunk from death, but bravely to the last fought about their King, guarding his person, and protecting him from danger (see **Note 40**). Life was cheerfully given up in his defence by bishops, earls, lords, and knights; and the field was honoured with the dust of the noble dead, and saturated with the best and bravest blood of Scotland.—(See **Note 41**.)

The English shafts in volleys hailed,
In headlong charge their horse assailed;
Front, flank, and rear, the squadrons sweep
To break the Scottish circle deep,
That fought around their King.

43

, though thick the shafts as snow.
...ugh charging knights like whirlwinds go,
Though billmen ply the ghastly blow,
Unbroken was the ring;
The stubborn spearmen still made good
Their dark impenetrable wood,
Each stepping where his comrade stood,
The instant that he fell.
No thought was there of dastard flight;
Linked in the serried phalanx tight,
Groom fought like noble, squire like knight.
As fearlessly and well.

Never in any engagement do we read of such havoc amongst the leaders of an army, excepting when Hannibal fought with the Roman consul, Varro; it was, in fact, the Scottish Cannae. Scarcely any family of note throughout the length and breadth of the land who had not to mourn over the death of a father, a husband, a son, or a brother. Most nobly did they fulfil their sacred vows made on the Borough Moor, that they would defend their King with the last drop of their blood (see **Note 42**). Had they been less precipitate in the encounter with Surrey's host, and more cautious in singling out, as their special foe, the commanders of the respective divisions of their enemy, in all probability there would have been as great a slaughter amongst the English nobility as there was in the Scotch (see **Note 43**).

The massing of the nobles about the person of the King, although done with the heroic intention of saving him from the sword of his enemy at the sacrifice of their own lives, tended to the fearful result of drawing together the fighting strength of the bill and bow men. It was on this point that James and his lords so vastly erred, for it finally led to the sad catastrophe of being hemmed in by the common soldiers of Surrey, who eagerly strove to cut down so noble a foe, especially when they found them resolutely determined to conquer or die on the very ground where hundreds of both armies lay drenched in their gory bed of death.

The battle continued from four to eight o'clock, or till darkness closed over the field of blood and carnage. Night alone put an end to the strife, for the combatants were only separated when they could not distinguish friend from foe. Numbers of the slain were stripped naked during the night, especially those who could be recognised by their armour as belonging to the nobles. The King, as well as his lords, underwent the same degradation; there was no escaping the plundering propensities of the Borderers, both English and Scotch, and also of the men of Teviotdale and Tynedale. Bishop Ruthal, in his letter, when speaking of the Borderers, says, in the quaint language of the time:

> The grettyst difficltie that I see therien is this, that such men of warre as shal be sent to the Borders, dow not trust the Borderers, whiche be falser than Scotts, and have done more harme at this tyme to our folks than the Scotts dyd, and therefor if it wer Goddys pleasure and the kyngs, I wold all the horsmen on the Borders were in Fraunce with you; for as I have wretyn byfore, they neve lyghtyd fro thayr horses, but when the bataylis joyned, than fell to ryflyng and robbying as well on our syde as of the Scotts.

There are various conflicting accounts recorded respecting the King's body, many of them bordering on the marvellous. It was the age of credulity and superstition; nothing remarkable could take place unless it were shrouded in mystery. Every event bearing on the King's death, let it be of what nature it may, had its supporters and propagators; and the more it bore the resemblance to a preposterous origin, the more it was revered and cherished throughout Scotland. By many it was believed that he did not fall in the battle; that he was seen, in the twilight of that eventful day, crossing the Tweed in company with four other horsemen; and by many it was firmly credited that he had gone as a pilgrim to the Holy Land.

By others it was affirmed that his body was found the day after the battle on the field, dreadfully mutilated, and that it was recognised by several who were well acquainted with his person. These various reports bear strong evidence that none of them could be relied upon with any degree of certainty; nor, even at this day, does history satisfactorily enlighten us on the subject There is, however, no doubt that he fell on the field, and in all probability was buried amongst the slain (see **Note 44**). Stripped of his armour, despoiled of all decorations belonging to his rank, covered with wounds, clotted with gore, and besmeared with blood, it would be almost impossible to distinguish him, with any degree of certainty, amongst the wreck and ruin of so great a number of naked dead.

> *What of them is left to tell*
> *Where they lie, or how they fell?*
> *Not a stone on their turf, not a bone in their graves,*
> *But they live in the verse that unmortally saves.*
>
>   Byron's *Siege of Corinth.*

From 10,000 to 12,000 fell on the field (see **Note 45**) with their King, and we may rely that nearly as many, if not an equal number, fell on the side of the English, for who ever heard of a Scotchman being in battle without leaving indelible proofs that he had been there? It was the tug of Greek with Greek, and we may almost affirm that no quarter was either given or taken; every one fought to the last—even the devotedness of Leonidas and his Spartan band at Thermopylae did not surpass the ardour and heroic valour of the King and those around him.

From such a number of slain we may judge pretty accurately the number engaged in the battle. Scotland on the Borough Moor counted 100,000 men; but certainly many of these returned home laden with plunder before the day of battle. Bishop Ruthal mentions that 20,000 returned to their own country, after the taking of Norham Castle. Lindsay of Pitscottie, in his account of Flodden Field, says that Lady Heron, in her letter to Surrey, diminishes the Scotch army to 10,000 men; and very shortly after, the same historian mentions that the vanguard was given to Huntly and Home, who were in number 10,000 men, and the King took the great battle unto himself, with all the nobility of Scotland, which passed not above 20,000 men. These conflicting and contradictory statements are of very little value; indeed, after all, we must draw our own conclusions from the different circumstances bearing more particularly on the event, Scotland, we know, mourned for her dead from the palace to the humble cot; and England's forces were so shattered, crippled, and diminished in this fearful battle, that she durst not attack or invade the territory of her foe. Both nations withdrew from the bloody strife terribly cut up and thinned in numbers, and not till the next day was it known which side was the victor.

We shall not, therefore, err far from the truth, when we assign to the different armies, at the commencement of the battle, something more than 40,000 (see **Note 46**) each, besides horse-soldiers, which in all probability would not be far from 4000 or 5000. The Borderers alone could muster strong in this arm of the service, for they prided themselves in being inured to war from their boyhood, and always ready for the fray. Look at Lord Home's party, called together in a few hours to avenge the aggression of the English, a short time previous to the battle. The King had only been a few weeks on English ground, and we know when he passed the Tweed his army consisted of 100,000 men.

Such slaughter and carnage could not possibly be inflicted in so short a time by a less number; and we cannot, upon calm reflection, but conclude that we are correct in assigning to each army the figures stated above. The effect of the battle was felt for generations after; and even at this day, (at time of first publication), in Scotland, Flodden Field cannot be mentioned without a sensation of terror and sorrow (see **Note 47**). Sir Walter Scott remarks that there is scarcely a Scottish family of eminence who does not number an ancestor killed at Flodden:

To town and tower, to down and dale,
To tell red Flodden's dismal tale,
And raise the universal wail.
Tradition, legend, tune, and song,
Shall many an age that wail prolong:

Still from the sire the son shall hear
Of the stern strife, and carnage drear.
Of Flodden's fatal field,
Where shivered was fair Scotland's spear.
And broken was her shield!

Scotland wept and mourned her King and nobility; her bards sang her loss in plaintive strains, and England in descriptive verse. He was the most beloved monarch that ever filled the Scottish throne. "As he was greatly beloved while alive," says Buchanan, "so, when dead, his memory was cherished with an affection beyond what I have ever read or hoard of being entertained for any other King" (see **Note 48**). More poetry has been written about Flodden Field than any other battle since the days of Homer. Scott has immortalised Flodden in his inimitable poem of *Marmion*, every part of which bearing on the battle can be read over and over again, without in the least degree diminishing the grandeur and excitement that enthrals the heart when first read, and which will continue to captivate and delight the soul of everyone who understands the English language.

The morning after the battle, the men under Lord Home were seen standing on the western end of the field where they had the evening before been so hotly engaged, and where they had been completely victorious (see **Note 49**). The centre of the Scotch had never been broken, and it was quite uncertain during the night which nation could claim the victory; but, as the day advanced, the Scotch left the ground and all their guns on the top of the hill.

The death of the King, together with the loss of nearly all the nobility who fought in the battle, would be known during the night, or early the next morning, throughout the remnant of the Scottish army. Besides the King, and his natural son, the Archbishop of St Andrews, there were slain twelve earls, and fifteen lords and chiefs of clans; and to these we must also add the Bishop of Caithness and of the Isles, the Abbots of Inchaffray and Kilwinning, and the Dean of Glasgow.—(See **Note 50**.)

When known in the English camp that the victory was theirs,

Surrey immediately ordered solemn thanksgiving to be offered up to the Almighty, and afterwards he created forty knights on the field, disbanded the remnant of his army, and returned to London, where all was joy and exultation.

Scarcely any one of note belonging to the English nobility fell on the field, which is a strong and undeniable proof that they did not risk their lives in the battle as the King and his nobles had done. The bow and the bill, in the hands of the English yeomen, did the deadly work, and by them were

The flowers of the forest a' wede away.

—(See **Note 51**.)

Notes

No. 1.—Surrey was made Lord High Treasurer *A.D.* 1501, and accompanied Margaret, the King's daughter (Henry VII.), a beautiful princess, at the age of fourteen years, with a great company of lords, ladies, knights, and squires, to the town of Berwick, whence she was conveyed to St Lambert's Church, in Lamyrmoor, where King James, attended by the chief nobility, received her, and carried her to Edinburgh. The next day after her arrival there, she was with great solemnity married unto him, in the presence of all his nobles.

The King gave great entertainments to the English, whom the Scotch noblemen and ladies far outshone both in costly apparel, rich jewels, massy chains, *habiliments* set with goldsmiths' work, garnished with pearls and stones of price, and in gallant and well-trapped horses. They made also great feasts for the English lords and ladies, and shewed them justing and other pleasant pastimes, as good as could be devised, after the manner of Scotland. Diverse ladies of Queen Margaret's train remained in Scotland, and were afterwards well married to noblemen.—Lesley; Hollinshed.

Queen Margaret's portion was £10.000, her jointure from King James £2000 a-year, and she received pin-money from him annually, £331, 6s. 8d. Ker marriage-portion, according to the present value of our money, (as at time of first publication), would be about £100,000, and her jointure £20,000 *per annum*. A curious account of the marriage of James IV. and Margaret occurs in Leland's *Collectanea*,

No. 2.—The Borough Moor in those days, according to Drummond of Hawthornden, was "a field spacious, and delightful by the shade of many stately and aged oaks." Upon this and similar occasions the royal standard is traditionally said to have been displayed from "The Harestone," a large stone now built in the wall on the left hand of the highway leading towards Braid, not far from Bruntsfield Links.—*The Pictorial History of Scotland.*

No. 3.—Hollinshed mentions that 500 or 600 were slain by Sir William Bulmer's forces, and 400 taken prisoners; whereas Buchanan, from whom I quote, estimates the prisoners at 200. He says that the invaders divided their plunder in the enemy's country, and each proceeded home with his portion by the nearest route; that it was the rear which fell into the ambuscade, and that the plunder which had been sent on before arrived safely in Scotland.

No. 4.—"In 1512," says Mr Fraser Tytler, the accomplished historian of Scotland—"to whose *Lives of Scottish Worthies* I refer you," says Lord Lindesay, "for a full and very interesting memoir of the Lyon-King,"—

> .... he was appointed servitor or gentleman-usher to the Prince, afterwards James V., and in the succeeding year he makes his appearance on a very strange and solemn occasion. He was standing beside the King in the Church of Linlithgow, when that extraordinary apparition took place (immediately before the battle of Flodden) which warned the monarch of his approaching danger, and solemnly entreated him to delay his journey. The scene is thus strikingly described by Pitscottie. 'The King,' says the author, 'came to Linlithgow, where he happenit to be for the time at the council, very sad and dolorous, making his devotion to God to send him good chance and fortune in his voyage.
> And there came ane man, clad in a blue gown, in at the kirk-door; beltit about him with a roll of linen cloth, a

pair of bootikins on his feet, to the great of his legs, with all other clothes conform thereto; but he had nothing on his head but syde red-yellow hair behind, and on his haffets [temples], which wan [reached] down to his shoulders, but his forehead was bald and bare. He seemed to be ane man of fifty years, with a great pike-staff in his hand, and came fast forward among the lords, crying and speiring [asking] for the King, saying that "he desirit to speak with him," while [till] at the last he came to the desk where the King was sitting at his prayers. But, when he saw the King, he made him little reverence or salutation, but leanit down familiarly on the desk before him, and said to him in this manner: "Sir King, my mother has sent me to thee, desiring thee not to go where thon art purposit; for, if thou do, thou shalt not fare weel in thy journey, nor none that are with thee. Further, she bade thee converse with no woman, nor use their counsel; for if thou do it, thou wilt be confounded and brought to shame."

By this man had spoken thir words to the King, the evensong was near done, and the King pausit on thir words, studying to give him an answer; but in the mean time, before the King's face, and in presence of all the haill lords that were about him for the time, this man evanishit away, as he had been ane blink of the sun, or an whip [a moment, or the smallest portion of time] of the whirlwind, and could no more be seen. I heard say Sir David Lindesay, Lyon-herald, and John Inglis, the marshal, who were at that time young men, and special servants to his Grace, were standing presently beside the King, who thought to have laid hands on this man, that they might have speirit further tidings at him, but all for nought; they could not touch him, for he vanishit away betwixt them, and was no more seen.'—Lord Lindesay's *Lives of the Lindesays*.

The wondering Monarch seemed to seek
For answer, and found none;
And when he raised his head to speak.

The monitor was gone.
The Marshal and myself had cast
To stop him as be outward passed;
But, lighter than the whirlwind's blast.
He vanished from our eyes,
Like sunbeam on the billow cast,
That glances but, and dies.
—Sir David Lindesay's Tale, *Marmion*.

No. 5.—There were assembled all his earls, lords, barons, and burgesses, and all manner of men between sixteen and sixty, spiritual and temporal, *burgh* and land, islesmen and others, to the number of 100,000; and reckoning carriage-men and artillery-men, who had the charge of fifty shot of cannons.—Pitscottie.

No. 6.—In defence of the broadsword generally used by the Highlandmen, we may instance the following as bearing testimony to its destructive effects, when wielded in the hands of men accustomed to fight with that weapon. General Stewart considers it even preferable to the bayonet, for he says:

> From the battle of Culloden, where a body of undisciplined Highlanders, shepherds and herdsmen, with their broadswords cut their way through some of the best disciplined and most approved regiments in the British army (drawn up on a field extremely favourable for regular troops), down to the time when the swords were taken from the Highlanders, the bayonet was in every instance overcome by the sword.'

In one of the skirmishes with the French in Egypt, a young sergeant of the 78th killed six of the enemy with the broadsword; the weapon was the same as that still used by sergeants in Highland regiments. The half-dozen Frenchmen were not cut down while retreating, but in fighting with the bayonet, hand to hand, by the broadsword. The gallant sergeant met his death-blow from a sabre-stroke from behind as he was returning to his company, after cutting down the last of his six foes.—"The Blue

Bonnets over the Border."—*Boys' Own Magazine,*

No. 7.—The Scots had twenty-two large brass cannon, and particularly seven of a very wide bore, all of the same size and make, called "The Seven Sisters," which the Earl of Surrey sent down to Berwick. According to the official report of the battle, they are described as "the neatest, the soundest, the best fashioned, the smallest in the touch-hole, and the most beautiful of their size and length that ever were seen."—Lambe.

No. 8.—Wilson, Alnwick, in his remarks on Northumberland castles, says of James IV., when invading England a short time before the battle of Flodden, that he besieged Norham, Wark, Etall, and Ford.

> There is, (says he), evidence of thirty-seven castles in Northumberland at the date of the civil wars between the houses of York and Lancaster, and architectural evidence of others. If we add to this list that the county likewise witnessed nineteen battles in the course of five centuries, besides the minor frays that were of everyday occurrence, we shall realise somewhat of the nature of the service performed by these stalwart fortresses, and of the military pomp and pageantry they saw and heard—the fluttering of pennons, glistening of arms, clattering of horses' hoofs, clinking of horses' trappings, resonance of war cries—in the days of their pride.

No. 9.—It is mentioned by Lambe, that there is a tradition here (at Norham) that King James, returning from a visit to Lady Heron at Ford Castle, found himself in danger of drowning in his passage through the Tweed near Norham, at the west ford, which is pretty deep on the Scotch side. Upon which he made a vow to the Virgin Mary, that if she would carry him safe to land, he would erect and dedicate a church (Lady Kirk) to her upon the banks of the Tweed, which he performed in the jubilee-year *a.d.* 1500, according to an old inscription on the church, now mostly defaced.

No. 10.—It appears from Madox's *Ecch.*, that Sir William Heron built the Castle of Ford in the year 1227, the estate having come into his family by an intermarriage with the heiress of Ford, who derived her descent from O'Donnel-de-Ford, who was seized of it in the reign of Henry I. This Sir William was governor of the castles of Bambrough, Pickering, and Scarborough, Lord Warden of the forest north of Trent, and Sheriff of Northumberland for eleven successive years. In the year 1335 the Scotch, under the Earls of Fife, March, and Douglas, making an inroad, destroyed the castles of Ford, Wark, and Cornhill.

Another of the same family, Sir William Heron, succeeded his brother John in the year 1498, being twenty years old. He was High Sheriff of Northumberland in the year 1526, and died in July 1535. He was twice married. By Elizabeth, his first wife, he had a son, William, who died before him; by the second, Agnes, he had no issue. It is uncertain which of the two was the redoubtable Lady of Ford at the time of the Battle of Flodden. Hall mentions the former.

In 1549 the Scots under D'Esse, a French general, laid the greater part in ashes, but were unable to reduce one of the towers, which was gallantly defended by Thomas Carr, formerly of Etall, who had married Elizabeth, the daughter of Margaret by her first husband. Sir William Heron, who inherited the castles and manors of Ford, Eshet, and Simonburn.—Willis's and Hutcheson's *Histories of Northumberland*.

No. 11.—The room in which King James slept a few days, or, as some affirm, the very night, previous to the battle, is still shewn in Ford Castle, and has now been fitted up and decorated in a manner worthy of its once kingly occupant. It is in the upper part of the south-west tower, looking in the direction of the Cheviot Hills and "dark Flodden's airy blow," where once stood the Scottish encampment, a distance of little more than a mile from the castle. Opposite the lodge on the Wooler road is a carriage-drive, nearly completed, which will encircle the whole of Flodden Hill, and on the west end approaches the rock, which is known by the name of "The King's Chair."

On either side trees and shrubs are planted, which in the course of a few years will render it one of the most interesting, attractive, and picturesque drives in the country. The well, close to the old encampment, from which King James and the Scottish army quenched their thirst, is to be restored, and a small stone basin inserted therein, and on Piper's Hill a monument will be erected, commemorative of the battle and supposed spot where the King fell. This celebrated Border castle, the seat of Louisa, Marchioness of Waterford, has undergone a thorough repair and enlargement, under the superintendence and refined taste of her Ladyship. The grounds about the gray castellated walls are laid out with special care and attention to command the splendid views that every turn in the undulated slopes affords.

The rich plain of Milfield, with its historic hills and British encampments, lies prominently in front, and the hold range of the Cheviot forms the far distant background of this enchanting landscape. Nowhere in the county of Northumberland can such a diversity of scenery be displayed. It embraces the low fertile valley through which the sullen Till winds its silent waters, and the trouting-stream of the glassy Glen, embosomed by the green peak of Yevering Bell, the Kirknewton Hills, and the lofty mountain-monarch of the district, from whose mossy summit, it is said, when the prospect is clear, may be seen the sea washing the eastern and western shores of merry old England.

Ever charming, ever new,
When will the landscape tire the view?
The mountain's fall, the river's flow,
The woody valley, warm and low—
The windy summit, wild and high,
Roughly rushing to the sky—
The pleasant dell, the mined tower.
The naked rock, the shady bower,
The town and village, dome and farm,
Each lends to each a double charm,
like pearls upon an Ethiop's arm.

There is another poet from whom I must be permitted to quote, before leaving this delightful subject. I allude to Robert Storey, who was born in the parish of Kirknewton, and brought up as a shepherd, and who has delineated the parts I have endeavoured to describe, in so happy and pleasing a manner. He thus speaks of the hilly country south of Ford Castle:

> '*These mountains wild,*' began the maiden, '*claim,*
> *Each for itself, a separate local name.*
> *We stand on Lanton Hill. Not far behind,*
> *The verdant Howsden woos the summer wind.*
> *That mountain, with its three wild peaks before.*
> *Is styled by dwellers near it Newton Torr,*
> *The oak-clad ridges there of Akeld swell.*
> *And here the bolder slopes of Yevering Bell.*
> *While towering yonder, with his patch of snow.*
> *And proudly overlooking all below,*
> *Is Cheviot's mighty self, his throne who fills,*
> *The admitted Monarch of Northumbrian hills.*'
> R. Storey, Guthrom the Dane.

No. 12.—When the Castle of Ford was stormed, Lady Heron, the wife of Sir William Heron, the castellan, who was a prisoner in Scotland, was taken prisoner; and, according to the Scottish historians Pitscottie and Buchanan, this beautiful and artful dame had such influence over the infatuated monarch, as to induce him to idle away his time till the opportunity of striking an effective blow against his enemy was irretrievably lost.

Ford Castle was the great barrier for the east march against Scotland. In a survey of the Borders in 1542 we have the following account of it:

> The Castle of Ford, standing likewise upon the east side of the said river of Till, was brunte by the last Kinge of Scots, a lytle before he was slayne at Flodden Field. Some parte thereof hathe bene reparetted againe sythence that tyme; but the great buyldings, and most necessarye houses, resteth ever sythens waste and decayed the which if they

were repared were able to receyve and lodge one hundreth and mo horsemen, to lye there in garrison in tyme of warre. And for that purpose, that is a place much convenient, and standeth well for servyce to be done at any place within the said east march, and ys of the inherytaunce of Sir William Heron's heyres.—Cotton MSS.

No. 13.—

The Earl, (according to Hall's account), forgat not to sende to all lords, spirituall and temporal, knyghtes, gentlemenne, or other which had tenaunts, or were rulers of townes or liberties (able to make men) to certifye what number of able men, horsed and harnesed, they were able to make within an houres wamynge, and to give their attendance on hym, and also he layed postes every waye, which postes stretched to the marches of Wales to the counseyll there, by reason whereof he had knowledge what was done in every coste.

No. 14.—It would appear that there were men from all parts of England in the army. John Winchcombe, the famous clothier of Newbury in Berkshire, commonly called "Jack of Newbury," was present in the battle, accompanied by a hundred of his own men, all armed and clothed at his expense.—*Vide* Lewis's *Topographical Dictionary of England*—see "Newbury." The kindling spirit of England's patriotism extended much farther than the northern counties. Boys even did what they could in the great cause of defence, for Henry Jenkins, about his eleventh year, who lived to be the oldest man upon record in England, was sent from the southern part of Richmondshire to Northallerton with a horse-load of arrows.—Lambe and White's *Flodden.*

No. 15.—According to the fashion of the previous reign, white was the prevailing colour of the whole army, save that of the mariners brought by the Admiral, and all wore the red cross of St George, except a dignitary of the Church, or an officer-at-arms.—White's *Flodden,*

No. 16.—Milfield, a small village where the Saxon kings of Berenicia, after the death of King Edwin, sometimes resided, on the south side of which is a spacious and beautiful plain, formerly overgrown with broom, famous for a defeat of a large body of Scots before the Battle of Branxton (Flodden) by Sir William Bulmer of Bromspath Castle, who commanded the forces of the bishopric of Durham.—Hollinshed, *Chron.*; Wallis.

No. 17.—Barmoor was the villa of the family of Muschampe in 1 Edward I., in 10 Elizabeth, and in 20 James I. of England. In this village, in 1418, the lords marchers of the northern counties were assembled with 100,000 men against the Scots, who retreated upon the report of such a mighty army.—Wallis.

No. 18.—The account given of Borthwick, the master-gunner, seems to me to be an idle tale, invented by the enemies of the King, *like many others* we read of in the history of this celebrated battle. The falling down on his knees, and imploring his royal master to permit him to fire upon the English whilst crossing the bridge at Twizel must have been a fabrication, circulated with the sole intention of defaming the private and military character of James, in making him appear ridiculously obstinate and fool-hardy to all good advice. It could not have been known in the Scottish camp more than a few hours before the battle commenced that the English had crossed the Till at Twizel.

They were then between five and six miles from the bridge, which was completely hid from their view; indeed, had they even seen the vanguard marching in that direction, which they could not possibly have done, it would have been impracticable to bring the cannon to bear upon the enemy, unless they had previously occupied the banks of the Till, which they did not. Lord Thomas Howard passed his artillery and men over it soon after ten o'clock a.m., and was more than four hours in bringing his guns and baggage-wagons from thence to the battlefield. Now for Borthwick to have transferred his heavy ordnance from the encampment at Flodden, or even from Branxton Hill, in those days in a shorter space of time, considering their ponderous weight, so as to tell effectually upon the enemy, is rather more than the most credulous could be brought to believe, especially if he had walked over the ground.

Indeed, the whole of this remarkable tale cannot, upon calm reflection, be regarded in any other light than of spurious origin, which, having been often repeated by those who were ignorant of the position of the ground, would at last be inserted by the historian as a fact, without considering the distance of the camp from the bridge, and the impossibility of the event.

No. 19.—John Heron, the Bastard, was son of John Heron of Ford, by a concubine. Having in an affray at a Border-meeting unfortunately killed Sir Robert Ker, warden of the middle marches, butler to James IV., and a great favourite with the king, he was outlawed in both kingdoms. Henry VII., to appease his son-in-law, delivered Sir William Heron of Ford to James, who kept him a prisoner in Fast Castle tower, in the Merse, on a rock above the Firth of Forth, until the battle of Flodden Field.—*Genealogical History of the Family of Heron.*

The Bastard Heron flourished many years, till *a.d.* 1524, when he, with 900 Englishmen, entered the marches of Scotland. After a stout battle with the Scots, 200 Englishmen were taken prisoners, and the Bastard slain.—Hollinshed.

Hall, as quoted by Lambe, mentions—

> Others write, that 200 Scots were taken, and that the rest fled, and that Sir Ralph Fenwicke, Leonard Musgrave, and the Bastard, with thirty other horsemen, having pursued the Scots too far, were overcome by them, Fenwick, Musgrave, and six others being taken prisoners, and the Bastard killed; whose death the Scotch thought to be a very ample recompense for the loss of their 200 men.

Many of the name of Heron were rectors of Ford previous to the battle; none after. Robert Heron, 1296.—King Edward I. granted his protection to Robert Heron, upon his giving a moiety of the profits of his living to him, a usual custom in those days. William Heron, Lawrence Heron, and John Heron-de-Ford-Arm. The latter was succeeded by Cuthbert Ogle, who was rector at the time of the Battle of Flodden, and Thomas Godergylle was vicar of Branxton.

No, 20.—It was at the confluence of the Leet, a small stream that encircles the lower part of the town of Coldstream, that General Monck drew up his forces previous to passing the ford on the Tweed, when about to march into England, immediately after the death of Cromwell. From the circumstance of Monck and his army being at this place, and, after his arrival in London, espousing the cause of royalty, the Coldstream Guards take their name, a regiment which ranks amongst the oldest in Her Majesty's service. Whilst speaking of this regiment, permit me to add the following testimony of its bravery from the pen of an enemy, in praise of the Coldstreams, which I copy from the *Times:*

> Todleben (the celebrated Russian general), in his defence of Sebastopol, when giving his account of the battle of Inkerman, mentions this regiment with every possible commendation for heroic courage. After describing in graphic terms this hard-contested battle, he goes on to say:
>> At first the skirmishers were repulsed by the English, but, supported by the Sappers of the 4th battalion, soon overthrew the English *tirailleurs*, and made way for the battalion at the head of the column. These then attacked with impetuosity the sandbag-battery, which was occupied by the worthy rivals of the regiment of Okhotsk, the intrepid Coldstreams. In spite of the concentrated fire of the Russian artillery on the left wing of our army, the Coldstreams received the attack with firm foot.
>> A bloody and obstinate combat ensued around the battery. Although still unfinished, the Coldstreams defended it, nevertheless, with as much tenacity as courage. The soldiers of Okhotsk scaled the parapets again and again, and even reached the interior of

the work, but they were repulsed every time, and could not establish themselves solidly. The combat at this point soon assumed the character of a hand-to-hand engagement. In the midst of the sanguinary *mêlée*, these intrepid soldiers carried on, one against the other, a terrible merciless struggle.

Whatever came to hand, whatever could injure an enemy, seemed fit for the combat. The soldiers changed shots with muzzles touching, struck each other with butts, fought bayonet to bayonet, and even threw stones and fragments of arms at each, other. At last, after unheard-of efforts to conquer such an energetic resistance, the soldiers of Okhotsk succeeded in expelling the Coldstreams from the battery and seizing it.

Nine guns were the reward of this brilliant feat of arms. Three were immediately taken away down the ravine, and the others were spiked Of 600 Coldstreams who defended the battery, 200 were *hors de combat*, but the regiment of Okhotsk bought the brilliant victory dearly. It lost its commander, Colonel Bebikow, who was mortally wounded, the greater part of its officers, and a very great number of soldiers..... Afterwards the remains of the Guards, having the Coldstreams at their head, again, attacked the battery, and once more drove the regiment of Okhotsk out of the works, and kept possession of it the remainder of the day.

No. 21.—The name of this small stream takes its origin from Paulinus, who baptised in this place, and also at Yeverin in Glendale, near Coupland Castle, in or about the year *a.d.* 627. In Yeverin, it is said that the number of people who flocked to him was so great, that for six-and-thirty days he was engaged from morning till evening in giving them daily instruction. When they could answer to the catechism he taught, they were baptised in the little River Glen, "for as yet there were no houses of prayer or baptisteries built," says Rede, "in the first years of the infant Church."

No. 22.—In almost all the accounts published immediately after the battle, the name of Brankston or Brampton was generally used to signify the place on which the battle was fought; and in many of the ancient songs the same name is given to it. Even so great an authority as Sir Walter Scott mentions that it ought to have been called the Battle of Branxton, and not Flodden. The village of Branxton is distant a little more than a mile and a half from the old encampment on Flodden Hill; And most undoubtedly the battle was fought to the east and west of the village, also in the vicinity of the church, and around the south side of the eminence we now think proper to call "Piper's Hill," which is only a few hundred yards from the church door.

> *At Flodden Field the Scots came in,*
> *Which made our English men fain;*
> *At Bramston Green this battle was seen.*
> *There was King James slain.*
>
> —From an ancient ballad, said to be given from the History of John Winchcomb, otherwise called Jack of Newbury, written by the Commons of England soon after the battle.

No. 23.—In a note appended to Hall's account of the battle, it is mentioned:

> The English army while on the march formed two large bodies, the forward and the rearward, commanded by the Lord Admiral, and his father, the Earl of Surrey. Each division had two wings—*viz*. The Lord Admiral, on the right Sir Edmond Howard, and on his left Sir Marmaduke Constable; the Earl of Surrey, on the right Lord Dacre, and on the left Sir Edward Stanley. The attack seems to have been led on in the same order, though after the Lord Admiral requested his father's aid, the rear advanced and left the forward, under the Lord Admiral, to the right.

Lord Dacre, however, kept his situation, which during the march was immediately behind Sir Edmond Howard, whence he, and under his orders Bastard Heron, were enabled to relieve Sir Edmond when discomfited by Home. We are not so clear where Sir Marmaduke Constable fought, and whether his corps was joined to that of the Admiral or of Sir Edward Stanley. The former is more probable, though as his body formed during the march, as it were, the van of Sir Edward, the latter supposition is by no means impossible. It was principally the difference between the order of marching and that of the battle which has confused the historians so much.

No. 24.—Something of a similar occurrence in our own time, as regards the wholesale slaughter of a company of men, has just taken place in America, which I copy from the *Scotsman*, June 13, 1864, headed "Swiss in the Federal Service."

> A letter from Switzerland says that information has been received from New York, that a company of 150 men, all Swiss by birth, and forming part of the 9th New York Regiment, commanded by a Swiss named Maesch, was destroyed to a man by the Confederates at the Battle of the Wilderness. Owing to the loss of the muster-rolls, and the death of Colonel Maesch, who alone knew all his countrymen by name, the War Department is unable to give any account of the fallen Swiss.

No. 25.—

> (Hollinshed) attributes this manoeuvre to the generalship of James, who, having determined to descend from his impregnable camp on the mountain of Flodden and give battle to the Earl, obtained possession of an advantageous eminence, which the Earl seemed desirous to occupy. It was probably the same hill from which Lennox and Argyle were dislodged by Sir Edward Stanley."

This hill could be no other than Branxton Hill.

No. 26.—Thus the two armies met, according to the old poem, on 'Flodden Field,' which so admirably points out the position of the English east and west of the village of Branxton, with their faces set southward, and the Scotch drawn up in position on Branxton Hill, pressing northward to meet their foe:

The English line stretched east and west,
And southward were their faces set;
The Scottish northward proudly prest,
And manfully their foes they met.

No. 27.—A cannon-ball weighing 13½ lb., now in the possession of Watson Askew, Esq., Pallinsburn, was found a few years since, (as at time of first publication), by one of my parishioners, when draining the upper or west end of Pallinsburn bog. May not this shot have been fired by the Scotch when the right division of Surrey's army was marching in the direction of Branxton, immediately after leaving the Wooler road? or it might have passed over the heads of the English after the battle had begun? Another ball, in the possession of John Collingwood, Esq., Cornhill House, was dug up since my residence in the parish, near the spot where such a number of human bones were found, about the year 1817, by Mr Rankin, now my churchwarden, when draining that part of the land, close to the ground taken up by the right wing under the command of the Lord Admiral and his brother Sir Edmond Howard, and where Home and Huntly fought

Both these balls are lead. I have in my possession two iron balls and a leaden one, turned up at different times by men ploughing or draining. The two iron ones were found, one on the side of the hill, the other over it, on which the Scotch took up their position, and the leaden one to the south-west of Piper's Hill. I have also a silver coin of Henry VIII., in an excellent state of preservation, picked up by a young woman residing in the village a few years ago, (as at time of first publication), when working on the land, which evidently had lain on the field ever since the battle. It was found to the south, a few hundred yards from the top of what is now considered to be Piper's Hill, a little to the south-west of the church.

May we not regard this coin as a silent witness, pointing out the exact position of the battle field? Another circumstance bearing on this important point, and which is well worthy of observation, is, that when widening the pathway leading to the church door, we came on a deposit of bones close to the surface. I counted several skulls within the space of four or five feet square, heaped one on the other. I can give no reason for these bones being found in such a position, unless we consider them as the remains of some of the heroes who fell in the village and about the church, hurriedly collected together and buried in a hole hastily dug for that purpose, that they might rest in consecrated ground. My churchyard is remarkably dry.

No. 28.—Alluding to this circumstance in the battle, the old ballad on *Flodden Field* describes it thus:

With whom encountered a strong Scot,
Which was the King's chief chamberlain,
Lord Home by name, of courage hot.
Who manfully marched them again.
Ten thousand Scots, well tried and told.
Under his standard stout he led;
When the Englishmen did them behold.
For fear at first they would have fled.

No. 29.—The descendants of these men fought at Culloden, and ever since then they have covered themselves with honour on every battlefield whereon they have been engaged. The following incident is copied from "The Blue Bonnets over the Border," written by an army chaplain, and published in an excellent little work entitled *The Boys' Own Magazine*. I quote it merely as shewing the high character of the Highland soldier, and the deep sense of honour felt by that mountain race when considered in the least degree slighted or degraded by a Superior.

Two men of gentle birth, privates in the Black Watch (afterwards the 42nd Regiment, equal in every respect to the 10th Legion of Caesar), were presented to George II. in 1743. 'They performed,' says the *Westminster Journal*, 'the broadsword exercise, and that of the Lochaber axe or lance, before His Majesty, the Duke of Cumberland, Marshal Wade, and a number of general officers assembled for the purpose in the great gallery of St James's. They displayed so much dexterity and skill in the management of their weapons, as to give perfect satisfaction to His Majesty. Each got a gratuity of one guinea, which they gave to the porter at the palace gate as they went out, and this not that they were dissatisfied with the gift, or that their purses were over well plenished, but they could not have accepted money without forfeiting their own respect, and their position as gentlemen.'

The following anecdote is also from the same author:

The 92nd or Gordon Highlanders was raised in 1794, by the last Duke of Gordon, then Marquess of Huntly, and by his mother, the beautiful and witty Duchess Jane. The Duchess used to frequent the country fairs, and when she saw a likely youth, she would try every persuasion to induce him to enlist. When all other arguments failed, she would place a guinea between her lips, and no young Highlander, however pacific, could refuse the bounty thus proffered. One kiss from that beautiful mouth was worth dying for.

No. 30.— Sir David Home of Wedderburn and his eldest son George were killed in the battle. His other sons were David (who succeeded to the title and estates), Alexander, John, Robert, Andrew, and Patrick. At the time of the battle they were called "The Seven Spears of Wedderburn." In all probability the father and son fell in this charge, which must have been made about the same time that Stanley was closing on the rear of the King. Home and Huntly could not but have witnessed, from, the position they were in, that the Cheshire and Lancashire men were hastening to the struggle.

They were fiercely engaged with the right wing of the English, and forcing them back on their centre, when Lord Dacre and the Bastard Heron, excited with the event—for they and their men must also have had a full view of Stanley's movements—rode rapidly forward, mingled with the combatants on the western end of the field, and effectually stopped the Highlanders and Borderers from advancing nearer the serried ranks of the men who, at this breathless moment, so nobly fought about their King. The standard carried in the battle, belonging to Sir David Home, is still kept, as a valuable relic of Flodden Field, in Wedderburn House, one of the seats of David Milne Home, Esq. of Milne Graden.

No. 31.—

The Earl, perceyuynge well the sainge of hys sonne, and seynge the Scottes ready to descende the hill, auaunsed himselfe and hys people forwarde, and brought them, equall on grounde with the forward on the left hande, even at the bront or breste of the same, at the foot of the hyll called Bramston; the English army stretched east and west, and their backes northe, and the Scotch on the southe before them, on the forsayde hyll called Bramston.—Hall's *Flodden*.

No. 32.—After introducing a speech of James to his army, Hollinshed proceeds with more spirit than his brother chronicler:

He had scarce made an end of his tale, but the soldiers, with great noise and clamour, cried: 'Forward! upon them!' shaking their weapons, in sign of an earnest desire they had (as then they shewed) to buckle with the Englishmen. Whereupon, without delaie, King James, putting his horse from him, all other nobles as meane men did the like, that the danger being equal, as well to the greatest as to the meanest, and all hope of succour taken awaie, which was to be looked for by flight, they might be the more willing to shew their manhood, sithe theii safety onelie rested in the edges and points of their weapons.

No. 33.—Scott, in his *Marmion*, when describing this part of the battle, says:

Far on the left, unseen the while,
Stanley broke Lennox and Argyle;
Though there the western mountaineer
Rushed with bare bosom on the spear.
And flung the feeble targe aside,
And with both hands the broadsword plied.

Sir Edward Stanley, the fifth son of Thomas, first Earl of Derby, commanded the rear at the Battle of Flodden, and with his Lancashire archers forced the right wing of the Scots from its advantageous position on the hill, and by this manoeuvre decided the battle. For these services he was, the following year, created Lord Monteagle, because his ancestors bore an eagle for their crest. He made a solemn declaration before he went to this battle that, if he returned victorious, he would do something to the honour of God; and accordingly on his return he began to build the magnificent chapel of Hornsby. In the chancel is an eagle cut in stone, with an inscription in Roman text: "*Edwardus Stanley, Miles, Dominus Monteagle, Me fieri fecit.*" Dying before it was completed, the parishioners finished the body of the chapel, which is of inferior workmanship.—Benson.

No. 34.—Alluding to this event in the battle, the old song, bearing the title of *Flodden Field*, sung by the Cornet and his men at Hawick, immediately after the marches have been ridden over, runs thus:

Bravely was the field defended,
Victory's palm was long suspended,
Till some English, like tornado,
Rushed from deepest ambuscado.

Now the struggle was unequal,
Dreadful carnage crowned the sequel;
Hardy Scots, borne down by numbers.
Strewed the field in death's cold slumbers.

No. 35.—The forces under Stanley, now brought to bear so destructively on the rear of the Scotch, were of the utmost importance to Surrey at this critical juncture, when victory seemed to have deserted the cause of the English The men under Lennox and Argyle, which composed the right wing, and which would amount to 10,000, if not more, had been fatally overthrown on the field, and forced to flee eastward, in the direction of Crookham.

Home was fully occupied in the west with the troops under his command. Surrey, the Lord Admiral, and Stanley, were now crowding with their forces about the King and his nobles, so that the Scotch must have been outnumbered by thousands on this part of the field at the close of the battle. The two wings, which could not have amounted to less than 20,000, were utterly unavailable to James and the resolute brave heroes who stood their ground and fought around him. Nothing could have been more detrimental to the success of the day; in fact, it was the crowning point of victory to the English.

Surrounded on all sides by overpowering numbers as with a living wall, from which death and destruction issued forth every fleeting moment, and men proclaiming, amidst the confused noise of battle and the last throes of life, that the day was won. Thus was Flodden Field lost to the Scotch, and this memorable Border battle, when almost within their grasp, was wrested from them by the overwhelming power that, at the last moment, rose as it were from every part of the field to seal their destruction, and complete their final overthrow.

No. 36.—

Eastward from Sir Edmond Howard was the Lord Admiyrall with his men, wyth whome encountred the Earles of Crafforde and Montrose, accompaygned with many lords, knightes, and gentlemen, all with spears on foote; but the Lords Admyrall and hys compaignie acquyted themselves so well, and that with pure fightyng, that thei brought to the ground a good number, and both the Earls slayne.—Hall.

Among those who fell on that disastrousp day, (says Lord Lindesay, in his *Lives of the Lindesays*), were our direct ancestor, the gallant young Walter of Edzell, and his chief, Earl John of Crawford, who conjointly with the 'gallant Graham' of that day, William, Earl of Montrose, commanded a dense body of 7000, or, according to the author of *Flodden Field*, 12,000 men, armed with long lances and leaden maces, which did great execution. They formed the second (from the left) of the four great divisions of the Scottish army, facing Thomas Howard, the Admiral, by whom, supported by Lord Dacre, they were routed and cut to pieces, though 'they did what they could to their utmost resistance, in hopes to have bathed their blades in English blood.'

I do not know, (says the same noble author), whether or not the old Lord of the Byres was personally engaged, but David of Kirkforther led his father's vassals to the field, and perished with his chief and King; of all his followers, but one single survivor returned to the 'bonnie parks of Garleton.'

For a' that fell at Flodden Field,
Bonny Hood of the Hule cam hame.
—Fragment of an old ballad, cited by Mr Miller—*Baldred of the Bass*, &c., 8vo, 1824.

No. 37.—
It is not to be doubted, (says the writer of the account of the battle printed by Richard Faques about 1515), that the Scottes fought manly, and were determined outher to Wynne the field or to dye. They were also as well

appoynted as was possyble at all poyntes with armoure and harneys, so that few of them were slayne with arrows. Howbeit the bylles dyd bete and hewe them downe with some payne and danger to Englysshemen. The sayd Scottes were too playnely determyned to abyde batayle, and not to flee, that they put off theyr bootes and shoes, and fought in the vampes of theyr hoses, every man for the most parte with a kene and a sharp spere of five yardes long and a target afore bim. And when theyr speies fayled, and were all spent, then they faught with great and sharpe swerdes makyng lytell or no noys.—Oliver's *Rambles in Northumberland*.

No. 38.—After the defeat of Lennox and Argyle, the centre under the King still maintained an obstinate and dubious conflict with the Earl of Surrey. The determined personal valour of James, imprudent as it was, had the effect of rousing to a pitch of desperate courage the meanest of the private soldiers; and the ground becoming soft and slippery from blood, they pulled off their boots and shoes, and secured a firmer footing by fighting in their hose.—Tytler's *History of Scotland*.

No. 39.—Nearly all agree, that when the King saw his standard-bearer, Sir Adam Foreman, fall, disdaining captivity, he pressed forward into the enemy's lines, and was slain. Several deadly wounds were inflicted upon him, especially one by an arrow, and another by a bill, which had opened the neck to the middle, while the left hand was almost cut off in two places.—Lambs; Godwin's *Annals*; Tytler.

No. 40.—Douglas, in his *Baronetage*, mentions that Hector Maclean of Dowart, who fought at the head of his clan, on perceiving his royal master in great danger from the English archers, interposed his body between His Majesty and them, and received several wounds of which he instantly died. Among the numerous instances of the melancholy effects of this destructive battle, the following is selected as one of the most striking:

In the reign of James IV. of Scotland, Andrew Pitcairn,

with his seven sons, went to the battle of Flodden, where they were all slain. The widow, who was left pregnant at home (she must have been a second wife), was delivered of a posthumous son, who continued the family. But, by the hardship of the times, they were both turned out of possession. Dr Archibald, the celebrated poet and physician, had, amongst the charters of the family, one from James V., restoring the widow to her jointure and the heir to his estate, with this honourable mention, that his father, with seven sons, had died on Flodden Field, fighting valiantly for his royal father.—*General Dictionary, Historial and Critical* (London, 1739).

No. 41.—George, Master of Angus, and William Douglas, the two sons of the old Earl of Angus, commonly called "Bell-the-Cat," together with two hundred gentlemen of the name of Douglas, fell in the battle. Hollinshed states that the aged Earl, broken-hearted at the calamities of his house and country, retired into a religious house where he died about a year after the Battle of Flodden.

No. 42.—In an old ballad, wherein the "Laird of Muirhead" is mentioned amongst twenty or thirty more, and which is now supposed to be lost, the following lines, said to be extracted from the said ballad, and kept by that family, may be quoted here as shewing the firm determination of the Scots to die or conquer on the field:

Afore the King in order stude
The stout laird of Muirhead,
Wi' that earn twa-handed muckle sword
That Bertram felled stark dead.

He sware he wadna lose his right
To fight in ilka field,
Nor budge him from his liege's sight
Till his last gasp should yield.

Twa hunder mair, of his own name,

Fra Torwood and the Clyde,
Sware they would never gang to hame,
But a' die by his syde.

And wondrons weil they kept their troth;
The sturdy royal band
Rushed down the brae wi' sic a pith.
That nane could them withstand.

Mony a bludey blow they delt.
The like was never seen;
And hadna that braw leader fallen
They ne'er had slain the King.

No. 43.—I shall give here in a note, taken from White's *Battle of Flodden*, a work to which I am greatly indebted, the names of a few of the English nobility, besides those I have already mentioned, who fought in the battle:

With Lord Thomas Howard and his brother, in the right wing, fought Richard Nevill, Lord Latimer, Lord Scrope of Upsal, Henry Lord Clifford, Thomas Lord Conyers of Sockburn, Sir Richard Cholmondsley of Cheshire, Sir William Percy, and others. Under the Earl of Surrey, in the centre, fought Sir Philip Tilney, Sir John Radcliffe of Lancashire, Sir John Mandeville, Sir Christopher Clapham, John Willoughby, &c. &c.; and in the east wing, on the left, under the command of Sir Edward Stanley, fought Sir William Molyneux of Sefton Hall in Cheshire, together with many of the nobility of Lancashire and Cheshire.

No. 44.—The pillar called the "King's Stone," situated a short distance from the Wooler road, a little to the north-west of the farm-onstead of Crookham West field, is usually, but erroneously, pointed out as the burying place of the King. This stone must have been in its present locality for years previous to the battle, and was anciently known as "the Gathering or Standing Stone on Crookham Moor." When England or Scotland intended to invade each other's country, the word was given for the soldiers to muster on such a day or night at "the Gathering-Stone on Crookham Moor." For this purpose it was made use of, thirty-two years after the battle, by the Earl of Hertford, when about to enter Scotland.

Had it been known in those days as the "King's Stone," he would never have designated it by any other name. This fact alone shews that its position and antiquity support an origin that dates a long time prior to Flodden Field. No doubt the Borderers on both sides of the Tweed have frequently gathered around its base before committing their nightly raids throughout the northern parts of England and the southern parts of Scotland. This stone may have been mentioned by Surrey, as well as the low moat of water which at that time lay between it and the village of Branxton, as the guiding points, south of which the van and the rear guards were to meet before the commencement of the battle.

No. 45.—

Of Scots lay slayne fall XII thousands,
And XI Earls, the soothe for to say;
XIII lords, and three bishops, as I understand,
With two abbots, which have learned a new play,
They should have been at home for peace to pray.
Wherefore they were thus wise punished by right:
So thy helpe, Lord, preservde our prince his right.
   —From an old ballad on the Battle of Brompton,

No. 46.—Lindsay of Pitscottie, after mentioning that Henry VIII. had sent a commission to the Earl of Surrey appointing him Lieutenant of the Northern Counties, says:

The Earl of Surrey, hearing the letters of commission presented by his son, was very rejoiced: and also of the homecoming of his son Lord Howard: and took such courage, that he assembled all his army of England, and made their numbers incontinent to the *number of fifty thousand gentlemen and commons.*

No, 47.—I shall insert here the beautiful Ode written by Dr Leyden after visiting the battlefield:

*Green Flodden, on thy blood-stained head
Descend no rain nor vernal dew,
But still, thou charnel of the dead,
May whitening bones thy surface strew.
Soon as I tread thy rush-clad vale,
Wild fancy feels the clasping mail,
The rancour of a thousand years
Glows in my breast: again I burn
To see the bannered pomp of war return,
And mark beneath the moon the silver light of spears.*

*Lo! bursting from their common tomb,
The spirits of the ancient dead
Dimly streak the parted gloom,
With awful faces, ghastly red,
As once around their martial king
They closed in death—devoted ring,
With dauntless hearts unknown to yield.
In slow procession round the pile
Of heaving corses, moves each shadowy file,
And chants the solemn strain, the dirge of Flodden Field.*

No. 48.—King James was killed in the twenty-fifth year of his reign, and the thirty-ninth of his age. He was of a majestic countenance, of a middle size, and strong body. By the use of exercise, a slender diet, and much watching, he could easily bear the extremities of weather, fatigue, and hunger. He excelled in fencing, shooting, and riding. He was of a high spirit, of easy access, courteous and mild; just in his juridical decisions, merciful in his punishments, which he inflicted upon offenders always unwillingly. He was poor from his profusion in sumptuous buildings, public shows, entertainments, and gifts.

As long as he lived he wore an iron-chain girdle about his body, to which he every year added one link, in testimony of his sorrow for having appeared at the head of the rebels who killed his father, James III., a.d. 1488, contrary to his express orders. It is said by Bishop Lesly, in his *History of James IV.*, that he was most warlike, just, and holy.—Lambs.

In Tytler's *History of Scotland* it is said that James had not completed his forty-second year when he fell on Flodden Field. In recording his character, he mentions that it was marked by very contradictory qualities. Although devoted to pleasure, wilful, and impetuous, he was energetic and indefatigable in the administration of justice, a patron of all useful arts, and laudably zealous for the introduction of law and order into the remotest parts of his dominions. The commerce and the agriculture of the country, the means of increasing the national security, the navy, the fisheries, the manufactures, were all subjects of interest to him; and his genuine kindness of heart, and accessibility to the lowest classes of his subjects, rendered him deservedly beloved. Yet he plunged needlessly into the miseries of war; and his thirst for individual honour, and an obstinate adherence to his own judgment, led to the sacrifice of his army and his life, and once more exposed the kingdom to the complicated evils of a minority.

No. 49.—Home has been grossly calumniated by his enemies for his conduct on the field; and even by some it has been alleged that he murdered the King in Home Castle. Why such grave charges should be brought against him it is impossible to conjecture, for nowhere can we find the least shadow of truth for such unfounded accusations. He was appointed chamberlain to the King, and Warden of the Marches, soon after his father's death, and he always continued the particular friend and favourite of James; in fact, he had every temporal good to lose, and nothing to gain, by the overthrow and death of his kind benefactor.

Being honourably chosen to the poet of danger, he led the van of the army, and in his impetuous attack carried all before him. He was the first to engage the enemy on the field, and the last to leave it. We have no instance of his antipathy to the King, or of his affection and friendship for the English. Born and bred a Borderer, he inherited all the hatred of the age for his foe, and previous to the battle was constantly engaged in the hazardous and important post of watching and guarding the boundary of the northern banks of the Tweed, and protecting his country from the sudden depredations of the English.

Certainly he defeated with great loss the troops under Sir Edmond Howard, amassed great plunder (for it was behind this division that the baggage-wagons were drawn up), and captured many prisoners, all of whom he managed to take with him into Scotland. He may have erred in not giving timely succour to the King, after having vanquished the light wing of the English, but he was never personally accused of this; and we must ever remember in his defence, that he commanded the Borderers—men who had always been accustomed to plunder their fallen foe in battle; and no doubt this pilfering propensity would be developed in the strongest manner, and with the keenest edge, on the field of Flodden. He fought with great bravery, and displayed great courage throughout the contest; and had it not been for Lord Dacre and the Bastard Heron holding him in check when on the point of engaging the troops under the Lord Admiral, he might have pushed his victorious Borderers to a further career of martial glory.

No one on the field could possibly have acquitted himself with greater devotion, or with more heroic enthusiasm to his King and country, than Home did; and if we may be permitted to judge from the carnage and overthrow of his enemy, none of Scotland's nobles did greater execution on the battlefield than he: indeed, we must confess that he was the only one of the northern lords who was victorious. Remaining on the spot defiant and triumphant, where he was surrounded by heaps of slain, he steadily kept possession of the ground throughout the night, and even threatened his enemy with a renewal of the contest the next morning; and no doubt, had he been supported by sufficient numbers, the Borderers would again, under their old commander, have once more combated with their English foe on the fatal field of Flodden.

No charge of cowardice or desertion was ever brought against him during his life; and history records that he rose to great power, and continued in great favour at the court of the infant king James V., till his opposition to Albany caused his exile. After his untimely and imprudent return, he was cited before the Scotch Parliament for his opposition to the intrigues of those in power, convicted of treason, and beheaded October 8, 1516.

Lord Dacre, in a letter to the English Council, dated 17th May 1514, and which I copy from the *Pictorial History of Scotland*, states that:

> ..... in the field of Branxston he and his friends encountered the Earl of Huntly and the Chamberlain; that Sir John Home, Cuthbert Home of Fast Castle, the son and heir of Sir John Home, Sir William Cockburn of Langton and his son, the son and heir of Sir David Home, the Laird of Blacater, and many others of Lord Home's kinsmen and Mends, were slain; and that, on the other hand, Philip Dacre, brother of Lord Dacre, was taken prisoner by the Scots, and many other of his kinsfolk, servants, and tenants were either taken or slain in the battle.

This statement completely disproves the charge against Home, that he remained inactive after defeating the division under Sir Edmond Howard.—Pinkerton.

No. 50.—The battle fought near Stamford Bridge between the Saxon Harold (who perished on the field of Hastings) and the Norway Harald Hardrada, is described by Creasy, in his *History of the Fifteen Decisive Battles of the World*, as equally fatal in respect to the slaughter of the flower of the Norwegian nobility as Flodden was to Scotland.

The Earls who fell on the field were Crawford, Montrose, Lennox, Argyle, Errol, Athol, Morton, Cassillis, Bothwell, Rothes, Caithness, and Glencairne. Amongst the number of the Lords and Chiefs of Clans we may mention Sir Duncan Campbell of Glennarchy, Sir Alexander Boswell of Balmuto, Sir William Douglas of Drumlanrig, Robert, third Lord Erskine, John, third Lord of Maxwell, besides others—*vide White's list of Scottish Noblemen and Gentlemen who were killed at Flodden Field*. Also five eldest sons of Peers, together with La Motto, the French ambassador and secretary to the King, who fought under Lennox and Argyle in the right wing. In this division fought the Campbells, Mackenzies, Macleods, Macleans, and other clans from the Highlands and Isles.

No. 51.—Had James been the obstinate and harsh master he is represented to have been by many of our ancient as well as modern historians, how must we account for the ardent affection and devotion shewn for his person in the day of battle? No danger was too great for his nobles and men to encounter when his life was at stake, and there is no one, not even his bitterest enemy, that can deprive him of, or refuse him, this honour. We cannot, then, but conclude with Buchanan, "that no king was more truly beloved by all ranks of his subjects than he." Such, I may almost say, unparalleled sacrifice of noble life, cannot be instanced in the history of any nation, when we regard the object and the cause that led to the carnage.

> *I never read in tragedy or story*
> *At ane journey so many nobles slain*
> *For the defence and love of their soverane.*
> Sir Dayid Lindesay.

He may have had his faults— for who can claim exemption?—but certainly, amiability of disposition, condescending manners, sincere friendship, heroic bravery, and genuine kindness of heart, were virtues not wanting in the character of James; and, to do him justice, we must not be too hasty in believing all the unfavourable and cruel speeches alleged against him, as having been uttered only a short time previous to the battle. Let him rest, beneath the sod on Flodden Field, in the sure and certain hope of Christian peace, and in the full blaze of military honour, where he most nobly did his duty as a king and a soldier, and where his ashes are surrounded by those intrepid and heroic spirits, who loved him better than life itself.

ALSO FROM LEONAUR
AVAILABLE IN SOFTCOVER OR HARDCOVER WITH DUST JACKET

THE ART OF WAR by Antoine Henri Jomini—Strategy & Tactics From the Age of Horse & Musket

THE MILITARY RELIGIOUS ORDERS OF THE MIDDLE AGES by F. C. Woodhouse—The Knights Templar, Hospitaller and Others.

THE BENGAL NATIVE ARMY by F. G. Cardew—An Invaluable Reference Resource.

THE 7TH (QUEEN'S OWN) HUSSARS: Volume 4—1688-1914 by C. R. B. Barrett—Uniforms, Equipment, Weapons, Traditions, the Services of Notable Officers and Men & the Appendices to All Volumes—Volume 4: 1688-1914.

THE SWORD OF THE CROWN by Eric W. Sheppard—A History of the British Army to 1914.

THE 7TH (QUEEN'S OWN) HUSSARS: Volume 3—1818-1914 by C. R. B. Barrett—On Campaign During the Canadian Rebellion, the Indian Mutiny, the Sudan, Matabeleland, Mashonaland and the Boer War Volume 3: 1818-1914.

THE CAMPAIGN OF WATERLOO by Antoine Henri Jomini—A Political & Military History from the French perspective.

THE AUXILIA OF THE ROMAN IMPERIAL ARMY by G. L. Cheeseman.

CAVALRY IN THE FRANCO-PRUSSIAN WAR by Jean Jacques Théophile Bonie & Otto August Johannes Kaehler—Actions of French Cavalry 1870 by Jean Jacques Théophile Bonie and Cavalry at Vionville & Mars-la-Tour by Otto August Johannes Kaehler.

NAPOLEON'S MEN AND METHODS by Alexander L. Kielland—The Rise and Fall of the Emperor and His Men Who Fought by His Side.

THE WOMAN IN BATTLE by Loreta Janeta Velazquez—Soldier, Spy and Secret Service Agent for the Confederacy During the American Civil War.

THE MILITARY SYSTEM OF THE ROMANS by Albert Harkness.

THE BATTLE OF ORISKANY 1777 by Ellis H. Roberts—The Conflict for the Mowhawk Valley During the American War of Independenc.

PERSONAL RECOLLECTIONS OF JOAN OF ARC by Mark Twain.

AVAILABLE ONLINE AT **www.leonaur.com**
AND FROM ALL GOOD BOOK STORES

ALSO FROM LEONAUR
AVAILABLE IN SOFTCOVER OR HARDCOVER WITH DUST JACKET

THE BATTLE OF BLOREHEATH by *Francis Randle Twemlow*—The First Major Conflict of the Wars of the Roses.

THE BATTLE OF THE FALKLAND ISLANDS by *H. Spencer Cooper*—The Royal Navy at War in the South Atlantic in the Early Days of the First World War.

THE NORMANS IN EUROPE by *Arthur Henry Johnson*—A History hof the 'Northmen' A.D. 700 to 1135.

CIVIL WAR EXPERIENCES by *Henry C. Meyer*—With the New York Cavalry Under Baynard, Gregg, Kilpatrick, Custer, Raulston & Newbury.

THE FIRST AND SECOND BATTLES OF NEWBURY AND THE SIEGE OF DONNINGTON CASTLE by *Walter Money*—During the English Civil War.

PARLIAMENT'S GENERALS OF THE ENGLISH CIVIL WAR 1642-1651 by *Neville Lloyd Walford*.

BRITAIN IN AFGHANISTAN 1: THE FIRST AFGHAN WAR 1839-42 by *Archibald Forbes*—From invasion to destruction-a British military disaster.

BRITAIN IN AFGHANISTAN 2: THE SECOND AFGHAN WAR 1878-80 by *Archibald Forbes*—This is the history of the Second Afghan War-another episode of British military history typified by savagery, massacre, siege and battles.

UP AMONG THE PANDIES by *Vivian Dering Majendie*—Experiences of a British Officer on Campaign During the Indian Mutiny, 1857-1858.

MUTINY: 1857 by *James Humphries*—Authentic Voices from the Indian Mutiny-First Hand Accounts of Battles, Sieges and Personal Hardships.

BLOW THE BUGLE, DRAW THE SWORD by *W. H. G. Kingston*—The Wars, Campaigns, Regiments and Soldiers of the British & Indian Armies During the Victorian Era, 1839-1898.

WAR BEYOND THE DRAGON PAGODA by *Major J. J. Snodgrass*—A Personal Narrative of the First Anglo-Burmese War 1824 - 1826.

THE HERO OF ALIWAL by *James Humphries*—The Campaigns of Sir Harry Smith in India, 1843-1846, During the Gwalior War & the First Sikh War.

ALL FOR A SHILLING A DAY by *Donald F. Featherstone*—The story of H.M. 16th, the Queen's Lancers During the first Sikh War 1845-1846.

AVAILABLE ONLINE AT **www.leonaur.com**
AND FROM ALL GOOD BOOK STORES

ALSO FROM LEONAUR
AVAILABLE IN SOFTCOVER OR HARDCOVER WITH DUST JACKET

THE FALL OF THE MOGHUL EMPIRE OF HINDUSTAN *by H. G. Keene*—By the beginning of the nineteenth century, as British and Indian armies under Lake and Wellesley dominated the scene, a little over half a century of conflict brought the Moghul Empire to its knees.

LADY SALE'S AFGHANISTAN *by Florentia Sale*—An Indomitable Victorian Lady's Account of the Retreat from Kabul During the First Afghan War.

THE CAMPAIGN OF MAGENTA AND SOLFERINO 1859 *by Harold Carmichael Wylly*—The Decisive Conflict for the Unification of Italy.

FRENCH'S CAVALRY CAMPAIGN *by J. G. Maydon*—A Special Correspondent's View of British Army Mounted Troops During the Boer War.

CAVALRY AT WATERLOO *by Sir Evelyn Wood*—British Mounted Troops During the Campaign of 1815.

THE SUBALTERN *by George Robert Gleig*—The Experiences of an Officer of the 85th Light Infantry During the Peninsular War.

NAPOLEON AT BAY, 1814 *by F. Loraine Petre*—The Campaigns to the Fall of the First Empire.

NAPOLEON AND THE CAMPAIGN OF 1806 *by Colonel Vachée*—The Napoleonic Method of Organisation and Command to the Battles of Jena & Auerstädt.

THE COMPLETE ADVENTURES IN THE CONNAUGHT RANGERS *by William Grattan*—The 88th Regiment during the Napoleonic Wars by a Serving Officer.

BUGLER AND OFFICER OF THE RIFLES *by William Green & Harry Smith*—With the 95th (Rifles) during the Peninsular & Waterloo Campaigns of the Napoleonic Wars.

NAPOLEONIC WAR STORIES *by Sir Arthur Quiller-Couch*—Tales of soldiers, spies, battles & sieges from the Peninsular & Waterloo campaigns.

CAPTAIN OF THE 95TH (RIFLES) *by Jonathan Leach*—An officer of Wellington's sharpshooters during the Peninsular, South of France and Waterloo campaigns of the Napoleonic wars.

RIFLEMAN COSTELLO *by Edward Costello*—The adventures of a soldier of the 95th (Rifles) in the Peninsular & Waterloo Campaigns of the Napoleonic wars.

AVAILABLE ONLINE AT **www.leonaur.com**
AND FROM ALL GOOD BOOK STORES

ALSO FROM LEONAUR
AVAILABLE IN SOFTCOVER OR HARDCOVER WITH DUST JACKET

AT THEM WITH THE BAYONET by *Donald F. Featherstone*—The first Anglo-Sikh War 1845-1846.

STEPHEN CRANE'S BATTLES by *Stephen Crane*—Nine Decisive Battles Recounted by the Author of 'The Red Badge of Courage'.

THE GURKHA WAR by *H. T. Prinsep*—The Anglo-Nepalese Conflict in North East India 1814-1816.

FIRE & BLOOD by *G. R. Gleig*—The burning of Washington & the battle of New Orleans, 1814, through the eyes of a young British soldier.

SOUND ADVANCE! by *Joseph Anderson*—Experiences of an officer of HM 50th regiment in Australia, Burma & the Gwalior war.

THE CAMPAIGN OF THE INDUS by *Thomas Holdsworth*—Experiences of a British Officer of the 2nd (Queen's Royal) Regiment in the Campaign to Place Shah Shuja on the Throne of Afghanistan 1838 - 1840.

WITH THE MADRAS EUROPEAN REGIMENT IN BURMA by *John Butler*—The Experiences of an Officer of the Honourable East India Company's Army During the First Anglo-Burmese War 1824 - 1826.

IN ZULULAND WITH THE BRITISH ARMY by *Charles L. Norris-Newman*—The Anglo-Zulu war of 1879 through the first-hand experiences of a special correspondent.

BESIEGED IN LUCKNOW by *Martin Richard Gubbins*—The first Anglo-Sikh War 1845-1846.

A TIGER ON HORSEBACK by *L. March Phillips*—The Experiences of a Trooper & Officer of Rimington's Guides - The Tigers - during the Anglo-Boer war 1899 - 1902.

SEPOYS, SIEGE & STORM by *Charles John Griffiths*—The Experiences of a young officer of H.M.'s 61st Regiment at Ferozepore, Delhi ridge and at the fall of Delhi during the Indian mutiny 1857.

CAMPAIGNING IN ZULULAND by *W. E. Montague*—Experiences on campaign during the Zulu war of 1879 with the 94th Regiment.

THE STORY OF THE GUIDES by *G.J. Younghusband*—The Exploits of the Soldiers of the famous Indian Army Regiment from the northwest frontier 1847 - 1900.

AVAILABLE ONLINE AT **www.leonaur.com**
AND FROM ALL GOOD BOOK STORES

ALSO FROM LEONAUR
AVAILABLE IN SOFTCOVER OR HARDCOVER WITH DUST JACKET

ZULU: 1879 *by D.C.F. Moodie & the Leonaur Editors*—The Anglo-Zulu War of 1879 from contemporary sources: First Hand Accounts, Interviews, Dispatches, Official Documents & Newspaper Reports.

THE RED DRAGOON *by W.J. Adams*—With the 7th Dragoon Guards in the Cape of Good Hope against the Boers & the Kaffir tribes during the 'war of the axe' 1843-48'.

THE RECOLLECTIONS OF SKINNER OF SKINNER'S HORSE *by James Skinner*—James Skinner and his 'Yellow Boys' Irregular cavalry in the wars of India between the British, Mahratta, Rajput, Mogul, Sikh & Pindarree Forces.

A CAVALRY OFFICER DURING THE SEPOY REVOLT *by A. R. D. Mackenzie*—Experiences with the 3rd Bengal Light Cavalry, the Guides and Sikh Irregular Cavalry from the outbreak to Delhi and Lucknow.

A NORFOLK SOLDIER IN THE FIRST SIKH WAR *by J W Baldwin*—Experiences of a private of H.M. 9th Regiment of Foot in the battles for the Punjab, India 1845-6.

TOMMY ATKINS' WAR STORIES: 14 FIRST HAND ACCOUNTS—Fourteen first hand accounts from the ranks of the British Army during Queen Victoria's Empire.

THE WATERLOO LETTERS *by H. T. Siborne*—Accounts of the Battle by British Officers for its Foremost Historian.

NEY: GENERAL OF CAVALRY VOLUME 1—1769-1799 *by Antoine Bulos*—The Early Career of a Marshal of the First Empire.

NEY: MARSHAL OF FRANCE VOLUME 2—1799-1805 *by Antoine Bulos*—The Early Career of a Marshal of the First Empire.

AIDE-DE-CAMP TO NAPOLEON *by Philippe-Paul de Ségur*—For anyone interested in the Napoleonic Wars this book, written by one who was intimate with the strategies and machinations of the Emperor, will be essential reading.

TWILIGHT OF EMPIRE *by Sir Thomas Ussher & Sir George Cockburn*—Two accounts of Napoleon's Journeys in Exile to Elba and St. Helena: Narrative of Events by Sir Thomas Ussher & Napoleon's Last Voyage: Extract of a diary by Sir George Cockburn.

PRIVATE WHEELER *by William Wheeler*—The letters of a soldier of the 51st Light Infantry during the Peninsular War & at Waterloo.

AVAILABLE ONLINE AT **www.leonaur.com**
AND FROM ALL GOOD BOOK STORES

ALSO FROM LEONAUR
AVAILABLE IN SOFTCOVER OR HARDCOVER WITH DUST JACKET

OFFICERS & GENTLEMEN *by Peter Hawker & William Graham*—Two Accounts of British Officers During the Peninsula War: Officer of Light Dragoons by Peter Hawker & Campaign in Portugal and Spain by William Graham.

THE WALCHEREN EXPEDITION *by Anonymous*—The Experiences of a British Officer of the 81st Regt. During the Campaign in the Low Countries of 1809.

LADIES OF WATERLOO *by Charlotte A. Eaton, Magdalene de Lancey & Juana Smith*—The Experiences of Three Women During the Campaign of 1815: Waterloo Days by Charlotte A. Eaton, A Week at Waterloo by Magdalene de Lancey & Juana's Story by Juana Smith.

JOURNAL OF AN OFFICER IN THE KING'S GERMAN LEGION *by John Frederick Hering*—Recollections of Campaigning During the Napoleonic Wars.

JOURNAL OF AN ARMY SURGEON IN THE PENINSULAR WAR *by Charles Boutflower*—The Recollections of a British Army Medical Man on Campaign During the Napoleonic Wars.

ON CAMPAIGN WITH MOORE AND WELLINGTON *by Anthony Hamilton*—The Experiences of a Soldier of the 43rd Regiment During the Peninsular War.

THE ROAD TO AUSTERLITZ *by R. G. Burton*—Napoleon's Campaign of 1805.

SOLDIERS OF NAPOLEON *by A. J. Doisy De Villargennes & Arthur Chuquet*—The Experiences of the Men of the French First Empire: Under the Eagles by A. J. Doisy De Villargennes & Voices of 1812 by Arthur Chuquet.

INVASION OF FRANCE, 1814 *by F. W. O. Maycock*—The Final Battles of the Napoleonic First Empire.

LEIPZIG—A CONFLICT OF TITANS *by Frederic Shoberl*—A Personal Experience of the 'Battle of the Nations' During the Napoleonic Wars, October 14th-19th, 1813.

SLASHERS *by Charles Cadell*—The Campaigns of the 28th Regiment of Foot During the Napoleonic Wars by a Serving Officer.

BATTLE IMPERIAL *by Charles William Vane*—The Campaigns in Germany & France for the Defeat of Napoleon 1813-1814.

SWIFT & BOLD *by Gibbes Rigaud*—The 60th Rifles During the Peninsula War.

AVAILABLE ONLINE AT **www.leonaur.com**
AND FROM ALL GOOD BOOK STORES

ALSO FROM LEONAUR
AVAILABLE IN SOFTCOVER OR HARDCOVER WITH DUST JACKET

ADVENTURES OF A YOUNG RIFLEMAN by Johann Christian Maempel—The Experiences of a Saxon in the French & British Armies During the Napoleonic Wars.

THE HUSSAR by Norbert Landsheit & G. R. Gleig—A German Cavalryman in British Service Throughout the Napoleonic Wars.

RECOLLECTIONS OF THE PENINSULA by Moyle Sherer—An Officer of the 34th Regiment of Foot—'The Cumberland Gentlemen'—on Campaign Against Napoleon's French Army in Spain.

MARINE OF REVOLUTION & CONSULATE by Moreau de Jonnès—The Recollections of a French Soldier of the Revolutionary Wars 1791-1804.

GENTLEMEN IN RED by John Dobbs & Robert Knowles—Two Accounts of British Infantry Officers During the Peninsular War Recollections of an Old 52nd Man by John Dobbs An Officer of Fusiliers by Robert Knowles.

CORPORAL BROWN'S CAMPAIGNS IN THE LOW COUNTRIES by Robert Brown—Recollections of a Coldstream Guard in the Early Campaigns Against Revolutionary France 1793-1795.

THE 7TH (QUEENS OWN) HUSSARS: Volume 2—1793-1815 by C. R. B. Barrett—During the Campaigns in the Low Countries & the Peninsula and Waterloo Campaigns of the Napoleonic Wars. Volume 2: 1793-1815.

THE MARENGO CAMPAIGN 1800 by Herbert H. Sargent—The Victory that Completed the Austrian Defeat in Italy.

DONALDSON OF THE 94TH—SCOTS BRIGADE by Joseph Donaldson—The Recollections of a Soldier During the Peninsula & South of France Campaigns of the Napoleonic Wars.

A CONSCRIPT FOR EMPIRE by Philippe as told to Johann Christian Maempel—The Experiences of a Young German Conscript During the Napoleonic Wars.

JOURNAL OF THE CAMPAIGN OF 1815 by Alexander Cavalié Mercer—The Experiences of an Officer of the Royal Horse Artillery During the Waterloo Campaign.

NAPOLEON'S CAMPAIGNS IN POLAND 1806-7 by Robert Wilson—The campaign in Poland from the Russian side of the conflict.

AVAILABLE ONLINE AT www.leonaur.com
AND FROM ALL GOOD BOOK STORES

ALSO FROM LEONAUR
AVAILABLE IN SOFTCOVER OR HARDCOVER WITH DUST JACKET

OMPTEDA OF THE KING'S GERMAN LEGION *by Christian von Ompteda*—A Hanoverian Officer on Campaign Against Napoleon.

LIEUTENANT SIMMONS OF THE 95TH (RIFLES) *by George Simmons*—Recollections of the Peninsula, South of France & Waterloo Campaigns of the Napoleonic Wars.

A HORSEMAN FOR THE EMPEROR *by Jean Baptiste Gazzola*—A Cavalryman of Napoleon's Army on Campaign Throughout the Napoleonic Wars.

SERGEANT LAWRENCE *by William Lawrence*—With the 40th Regt. of Foot in South America, the Peninsular War & at Waterloo.

CAMPAIGNS WITH THE FIELD TRAIN *by Richard D. Henegan*—Experiences of a British Officer During the Peninsula and Waterloo Campaigns of the Napoleonic Wars.

CAVALRY SURGEON *by S. D. Broughton*—On Campaign Against Napoleon in the Peninsula & South of France During the Napoleonic Wars 1812-1814.

MEN OF THE RIFLES *by Thomas Knight, Henry Curling & Jonathan Leach*—The Reminiscences of Thomas Knight of the 95th (Rifles) by Thomas Knight, Henry Curling's Anecdotes by Henry Curling & The Field Services of the Rifle Brigade from its Formation to Waterloo by Jonathan Leach.

THE ULM CAMPAIGN 1805 *by F. N. Maude*—Napoleon and the Defeat of the Austrian Army During the 'War of the Third Coalition'.

SOLDIERING WITH THE 'DIVISION' *by Thomas Garrety*—The Military Experiences of an Infantryman of the 43rd Regiment During the Napoleonic Wars.

SERGEANT MORRIS OF THE 73RD FOOT *by Thomas Morris*—The Experiences of a British Infantryman During the Napoleonic Wars-Including Campaigns in Germany and at Waterloo.

A VOICE FROM WATERLOO *by Edward Cotton*—The Personal Experiences of a British Cavalryman Who Became a Battlefield Guide and Authority on the Campaign of 1815.

NAPOLEON AND HIS MARSHALS *by J. T. Headley*—The Men of the First Empire.

AVAILABLE ONLINE AT www.leonaur.com
AND FROM ALL GOOD BOOK STORES

ALSO FROM LEONAUR
AVAILABLE IN SOFTCOVER OR HARDCOVER WITH DUST JACKET

COLBORNE: A SINGULAR TALENT FOR WAR by *John Colborne*—The Napoleonic Wars Career of One of Wellington's Most Highly Valued Officers in Egypt, Holland, Italy, the Peninsula and at Waterloo.

NAPOLEON'S RUSSIAN CAMPAIGN by *Philippe Henri de Segur*—The Invasion, Battles and Retreat by an Aide-de-Camp on the Emperor's Staff.

WITH THE LIGHT DIVISION by *John H. Cooke*—The Experiences of an Officer of the 43rd Light Infantry in the Peninsula and South of France During the Napoleonic Wars.

WELLINGTON AND THE PYRENEES CAMPAIGN VOLUME I: FROM VITORIA TO THE BIDASSOA by *F. C. Beatson*—The final phase of the campaign in the Iberian Peninsula.

WELLINGTON AND THE INVASION OF FRANCE VOLUME II: THE BIDASSOA TO THE BATTLE OF THE NIVELLE by *F. C. Beatson*—The final phase of the campaign in the Iberian Peninsula.

WELLINGTON AND THE FALL OF FRANCE VOLUME III: THE GAVES AND THE BATTLE OF ORTHEZ by *F. C. Beatson*—The final phase of the campaign in the Iberian Peninsula.

NAPOLEON'S IMPERIAL GUARD: FROM MARENGO TO WATERLOO by *J. T. Headley*—The story of Napoleon's Imperial Guard and the men who commanded them.

BATTLES & SIEGES OF THE PENINSULAR WAR by *W. H. Fitchett*—Corunna, Busaco, Albuera, Ciudad Rodrigo, Badajos, Salamanca, San Sebastian & Others.

SERGEANT GUILLEMARD: THE MAN WHO SHOT NELSON? by *Robert Guillemard*—A Soldier of the Infantry of the French Army of Napoleon on Campaign Throughout Europe.

WITH THE GUARDS ACROSS THE PYRENEES by *Robert Batty*—The Experiences of a British Officer of Wellington's Army During the Battles for the Fall of Napoleonic France, 1813.

A STAFF OFFICER IN THE PENINSULA by *E. W. Buckham*—An Officer of the British Staff Corps Cavalry During the Peninsula Campaign of the Napoleonic Wars.

THE LEIPZIG CAMPAIGN: 1813—NAPOLEON AND THE "BATTLE OF THE NATIONS" by *F. N. Maude*—Colonel Maude's analysis of Napoleon's campaign of 1813 around Leipzig.

AVAILABLE ONLINE AT **www.leonaur.com**
AND FROM ALL GOOD BOOK STORES

ALSO FROM LEONAUR
AVAILABLE IN SOFTCOVER OR HARDCOVER WITH DUST JACKET

BUGEAUD: A PACK WITH A BATON by *Thomas Robert Bugeaud*—The Early Campaigns of a Soldier of Napoleon's Army Who Would Become a Marshal of France.

WATERLOO RECOLLECTIONS by *Frederick Llewellyn*—Rare First Hand Accounts, Letters, Reports and Retellings from the Campaign of 1815.

SERGEANT NICOL by *Daniel Nicol*—The Experiences of a Gordon Highlander During the Napoleonic Wars in Egypt, the Peninsula and France.

THE JENA CAMPAIGN: 1806 by *F. N. Maude*—The Twin Battles of Jena & Auerstadt Between Napoleon's French and the Prussian Army.

PRIVATE O'NEIL by *Charles O'Neil*—The recollections of an Irish Rogue of H. M. 28th Regt.—The Slashers—during the Peninsula & Waterloo campaigns of the Napoleonic war.

ROYAL HIGHLANDER by *James Anton*—A soldier of H.M 42nd (Royal) Highlanders during the Peninsular, South of France & Waterloo Campaigns of the Napoleonic Wars.

CAPTAIN BLAZE by *Elzéar Blaze*—Life in Napoleons Army.

LEJEUNE VOLUME 1 by *Louis-François Lejeune*—The Napoleonic Wars through the Experiences of an Officer on Berthier's Staff.

LEJEUNE VOLUME 2 by *Louis-François Lejeune*—The Napoleonic Wars through the Experiences of an Officer on Berthier's Staff.

CAPTAIN COIGNET by *Jean-Roch Coignet*—A Soldier of Napoleon's Imperial Guard from the Italian Campaign to Russia and Waterloo.

FUSILIER COOPER by *John S. Cooper*—Experiences in the 7th (Royal) Fusiliers During the Peninsular Campaign of the Napoleonic Wars and the American Campaign to New Orleans.

FIGHTING NAPOLEON'S EMPIRE by *Joseph Anderson*—The Campaigns of a British Infantryman in Italy, Egypt, the Peninsular & the West Indies During the Napoleonic Wars.

CHASSEUR BARRES by *Jean-Baptiste Barres*—The experiences of a French Infantryman of the Imperial Guard at Austerlitz, Jena, Eylau, Friedland, in the Peninsular, Lutzen, Bautzen, Zinnwald and Hanau during the Napoleonic Wars.

AVAILABLE ONLINE AT www.leonaur.com
AND FROM ALL GOOD BOOK STORES

ALSO FROM LEONAUR
AVAILABLE IN SOFTCOVER OR HARDCOVER WITH DUST JACKET

CAPTAIN COIGNET by *Jean-Roch Coignet*—A Soldier of Napoleon's Imperial Guard from the Italian Campaign to Russia and Waterloo.

HUSSAR ROCCA by *Albert Jean Michel de Rocca*—A French cavalry officer's experiences of the Napoleonic Wars and his views on the Peninsular Campaigns against the Spanish, British And Guerilla Armies.

MARINES TO 95TH (RIFLES) by *Thomas Fernyhough*—The military experiences of Robert Fernyhough during the Napoleonic Wars.

LIGHT BOB by *Robert Blakeney*—The experiences of a young officer in H.M 28th & 36th regiments of the British Infantry during the Peninsular Campaign of the Napoleonic Wars 1804 - 1814.

WITH WELLINGTON'S LIGHT CAVALRY by *William Tomkinson*—The Experiences of an officer of the 16th Light Dragoons in the Peninsular and Waterloo campaigns of the Napoleonic Wars.

SERGEANT BOURGOGNE by *Adrien Bourgogne*—With Napoleon's Imperial Guard in the Russian Campaign and on the Retreat from Moscow 1812 - 13.

SURTEES OF THE 95TH (RIFLES) by *William Surtees*—A Soldier of the 95th (Rifles) in the Peninsular campaign of the Napoleonic Wars.

SWORDS OF HONOUR by *Henry Newbolt & Stanley L. Wood*—The Careers of Six Outstanding Officers from the Napoleonic Wars, the Wars for India and the American Civil War.

ENSIGN BELL IN THE PENINSULAR WAR by *George Bell*—The Experiences of a young British Soldier of the 34th Regiment 'The Cumberland Gentlemen' in the Napoleonic wars.

HUSSAR IN WINTER by *Alexander Gordon*—A British Cavalry Officer during the retreat to Corunna in the Peninsular campaign of the Napoleonic Wars.

THE COMPLEAT RIFLEMAN HARRIS by *Benjamin Harris as told to and transcribed by Captain Henry Curling, 52nd Regt. of Foot*—The adventures of a soldier of the 95th (Rifles) during the Peninsular Campaign of the Napoleonic Wars.

THE ADVENTURES OF A LIGHT DRAGOON by *George Farmer & G.R. Gleig*—A cavalryman during the Peninsular & Waterloo Campaigns, in captivity & at the siege of Bhurtpore, India.

AVAILABLE ONLINE AT **www.leonaur.com**
AND FROM ALL GOOD BOOK STORES

ALSO FROM LEONAUR
AVAILABLE IN SOFTCOVER OR HARDCOVER WITH DUST JACKET

THE LIFE OF THE REAL BRIGADIER GERARD VOLUME 1—THE YOUNG HUSSAR 1782-1807 *by Jean-Baptiste De Marbot*—A French Cavalryman Of the Napoleonic Wars at Marengo, Austerlitz, Jena, Eylau & Friedland.

THE LIFE OF THE REAL BRIGADIER GERARD VOLUME 2—IMPERIAL AIDE-DE-CAMP 1807-1811 *by Jean-Baptiste De Marbot*—A French Cavalryman of the Napoleonic Wars at Saragossa, Landshut, Eckmuhl, Ratisbon, Aspern-Essling, Wagram, Busaco & Torres Vedras.

THE LIFE OF THE REAL BRIGADIER GERARD VOLUME 3—COLONEL OF CHASSEURS 1811-1815 *by Jean-Baptiste De Marbot*—A French Cavalryman in the retreat from Moscow, Lutzen, Bautzen, Katzbach, Leipzig, Hanau & Waterloo.

THE INDIAN WAR OF 1864 *by Eugene Ware*—The Experiences of a Young Officer of the 7th Iowa Cavalry on the Western Frontier During the Civil War.

THE MARCH OF DESTINY *by Charles E. Young & V. Devinny*—Dangers of the Trail in 1865 by Charles E. Young & The Story of a Pioneer by V. Devinny, two Accounts of Early Emigrants to Colorado.

CROSSING THE PLAINS *by William Audley Maxwell*—A First Hand Narrative of the Early Pioneer Trail to California in 1857.

CHIEF OF SCOUTS *by William F. Drannan*—A Pilot to Emigrant and Government Trains, Across the Plains of the Western Frontier.

THIRTY-ONE YEARS ON THE PLAINS AND IN THE MOUNTAINS *by William F. Drannan*—William Drannan was born to be a pioneer, hunter, trapper and wagon train guide during the momentous days of the Great American West.

THE INDIAN WARS VOLUNTEER *by William Thompson*—Recollections of the Conflict Against the Snakes, Shoshone, Bannocks, Modocs and Other Native Tribes of the American North West.

THE 4TH TENNESSEE CAVALRY *by George B. Guild*—The Services of Smith's Regiment of Confederate Cavalry by One of its Officers.

COLONEL WORTHINGTON'S SHILOH *by T. Worthington*—The Tennessee Campaign, 1862, by an Officer of the Ohio Volunteers.

FOUR YEARS IN THE SADDLE *by W. L. Curry*—The History of the First Regiment Ohio Volunteer Cavalry in the American Civil War.

AVAILABLE ONLINE AT **www.leonaur.com**
AND FROM ALL GOOD BOOK STORES

ALSO FROM LEONAUR
AVAILABLE IN SOFTCOVER OR HARDCOVER WITH DUST JACKET

LIFE IN THE ARMY OF NORTHERN VIRGINIA by *Carlton McCarthy*—The Observations of a Confederate Artilleryman of Cutshaw's Battalion During the American Civil War 1861-1865.

HISTORY OF THE CAVALRY OF THE ARMY OF THE POTOMAC by *Charles D. Rhodes*—Including Pope's Army of Virginia and the Cavalry Operations in West Virginia During the American Civil War.

CAMP-FIRE AND COTTON-FIELD by *Thomas W. Knox*—A New York Herald Correspondent's View of the American Civil War.

SERGEANT STILLWELL by *Leander Stillwell*—The Experiences of a Union Army Soldier of the 61st Illinois Infantry During the American Civil War.

STONEWALL'S CANNONEER by *Edward A. Moore*—Experiences with the Rockbridge Artillery, Confederate Army of Northern Virginia, During the American Civil War.

THE SIXTH CORPS by *George Stevens*—The Army of the Potomac, Union Army, During the American Civil War.

THE RAILROAD RAIDERS by *William Pittenger*—An Ohio Volunteers Recollections of the Andrews Raid to Disrupt the Confederate Railroad in Georgia During the American Civil War.

CITIZEN SOLDIER by *John Beatty*—An Account of the American Civil War by a Union Infantry Officer of Ohio Volunteers Who Became a Brigadier General.

COX: PERSONAL RECOLLECTIONS OF THE CIVIL WAR--VOLUME 1 by *Jacob Dolson Cox*—West Virginia, Kanawha Valley, Gauley Bridge, Cotton Mountain, South Mountain, Antietam, the Morgan Raid & the East Tennessee Campaign.

COX: PERSONAL RECOLLECTIONS OF THE CIVIL WAR--VOLUME 2 by *Jacob Dolson Cox*—Siege of Knoxville, East Tennessee, Atlanta Campaign, the Nashville Campaign & the North Carolina Campaign.

KERSHAW'S BRIGADE VOLUME 1 by *D. Augustus Dickert*—Manassas, Seven Pines, Sharpsburg (Antietam), Fredricksburg, Chancellorsville, Gettysburg, Chickamauga, Chattanooga, Fort Sanders & Bean Station.

KERSHAW'S BRIGADE VOLUME 2 by *D. Augustus Dickert*—At the wilderness, Cold Harbour, Petersburg, The Shenandoah Valley and Cedar Creek..

AVAILABLE ONLINE AT **www.leonaur.com**
AND FROM ALL GOOD BOOK STORES

ALSO FROM LEONAUR
AVAILABLE IN SOFTCOVER OR HARDCOVER WITH DUST JACKET

THE RELUCTANT REBEL by William G. Stevenson—A young Kentuckian's experiences in the Confederate Infantry & Cavalry during the American Civil War..

BOOTS AND SADDLES by Elizabeth B. Custer—The experiences of General Custer's Wife on the Western Plains.

FANNIE BEERS' CIVIL WAR by Fannie A. Beers—A Confederate Lady's Experiences of Nursing During the Campaigns & Battles of the American Civil War.

LADY SALE'S AFGHANISTAN by Florentia Sale—An Indomitable Victorian Lady's Account of the Retreat from Kabul During the First Afghan War.

THE TWO WARS OF MRS DUBERLY by Frances Isabella Duberly—An Intrepid Victorian Lady's Experience of the Crimea and Indian Mutiny.

THE REBELLIOUS DUCHESS by Paul F. S. Dermoncourt—The Adventures of the Duchess of Berri and Her Attempt to Overthrow French Monarchy.

LADIES OF WATERLOO by Charlotte A. Eaton, Magdalene de Lancey & Juana Smith—The Experiences of Three Women During the Campaign of 1815: Waterloo Days by Charlotte A. Eaton, A Week at Waterloo by Magdalene de Lancey & Juana's Story by Juana Smith.

TWO YEARS BEFORE THE MAST by Richard Henry Dana. Jr.—The account of one young man's experiences serving on board a sailing brig—the Penelope—bound for California, between the years 1834-36.

A SAILOR OF KING GEORGE by Frederick Hoffman—From Midshipman to Captain—Recollections of War at Sea in the Napoleonic Age 1793-1815.

LORDS OF THE SEA by A. T. Mahan—Great Captains of the Royal Navy During the Age of Sail.

COGGESHALL'S VOYAGES: VOLUME 1 by George Coggeshall—The Recollections of an American Schooner Captain.

COGGESHALL'S VOYAGES: VOLUME 2 by George Coggeshall—The Recollections of an American Schooner Captain.

TWILIGHT OF EMPIRE by Sir Thomas Ussher & Sir George Cockburn—Two accounts of Napoleon's Journeys in Exile to Elba and St. Helena: Narrative of Events by Sir Thomas Ussher & Napoleon's Last Voyage: Extract of a diary by Sir George Cockburn.

AVAILABLE ONLINE AT **www.leonaur.com**
AND FROM ALL GOOD BOOK STORES

ALSO FROM LEONAUR
AVAILABLE IN SOFTCOVER OR HARDCOVER WITH DUST JACKET

ESCAPE FROM THE FRENCH by *Edward Boys*—A Young Royal Navy Midshipman's Adventures During the Napoleonic War.

THE VOYAGE OF H.M.S. PANDORA by *Edward Edwards R. N. & George Hamilton, edited by Basil Thomson*—In Pursuit of the Mutineers of the Bounty in the South Seas—1790-1791.

MEDUSA by *J. B. Henry Savigny and Alexander Correard and Charlotte-Adélaïde Dard* —Narrative of a Voyage to Senegal in 1816 & The Sufferings of the Picard Family After the Shipwreck of the Medusa.

THE SEA WAR OF 1812 VOLUME 1 by *A. T. Mahan*—A History of the Maritime Conflict.

THE SEA WAR OF 1812 VOLUME 2 by *A. T. Mahan*—A History of the Maritime Conflict.

WETHERELL OF H. M. S. HUSSAR by *John Wetherell*—The Recollections of an Ordinary Seaman of the Royal Navy During the Napoleonic Wars.

THE NAVAL BRIGADE IN NATAL by *C. R. N. Burne*—With the Guns of H. M. S. Terrible & H. M. S. Tartar during the Boer War 1899-1900.

THE VOYAGE OF H. M. S. BOUNTY by *William Bligh*—The True Story of an 18th Century Voyage of Exploration and Mutiny.

SHIPWRECK! by *William Gilly*—The Royal Navy's Disasters at Sea 1793-1849.

KING'S CUTTERS AND SMUGGLERS: 1700-1855 by *E. Keble Chatterton*—A unique period of maritime history-from the beginning of the eighteenth to the middle of the nineteenth century when British seamen risked all to smuggle valuable goods from wool to tea and spirits from and to the Continent.

CONFEDERATE BLOCKADE RUNNER by *John Wilkinson*—The Personal Recollections of an Officer of the Confederate Navy.

NAVAL BATTLES OF THE NAPOLEONIC WARS by *W. H. Fitchett*—Cape St. Vincent, the Nile, Cadiz, Copenhagen, Trafalgar & Others.

PRISONERS OF THE RED DESERT by *R. S. Gwatkin-Williams*—The Adventures of the Crew of the Tara During the First World War.

U-BOAT WAR 1914-1918 by *James B. Connolly/Karl von Schenk*—Two Contrasting Accounts from Both Sides of the Conflict at Sea D uring the Great War.

AVAILABLE ONLINE AT **www.leonaur.com**
AND FROM ALL GOOD BOOK STORES

ALSO FROM LEONAUR
AVAILABLE IN SOFTCOVER OR HARDCOVER WITH DUST JACKET

IRON TIMES WITH THE GUARDS *by An O. E. (G. P. A. Fildes)*—The Experiences of an Officer of the Coldstream Guards on the Western Front During the First World War.

THE GREAT WAR IN THE MIDDLE EAST: 1 *by W. T. Massey*—The Desert Campaigns & How Jerusalem Was Won---two classic accounts in one volume.

THE GREAT WAR IN THE MIDDLE EAST: 2 *by W. T. Massey*—Allenby's Final Triumph.

SMITH-DORRIEN *by Horace Smith-Dorrien*—Isandlwhana to the Great War.

1914 *by Sir John French*—The Early Campaigns of the Great War by the British Commander.

GRENADIER *by E. R. M. Fryer*—The Recollections of an Officer of the Grenadier Guards throughout the Great War on the Western Front.

BATTLE, CAPTURE & ESCAPE *by George Pearson*—The Experiences of a Canadian Light Infantryman During the Great War.

DIGGERS AT WAR *by R. Hugh Knyvett & G. P. Cuttriss*—"Over There" With the Australians by R. Hugh Knyvett and Over the Top With the Third Australian Division by G. P. Cuttriss. Accounts of Australians During the Great War in the Middle East, at Gallipoli and on the Western Front.

HEAVY FIGHTING BEFORE US *by George Brenton Laurie*—The Letters of an Officer of the Royal Irish Rifles on the Western Front During the Great War.

THE CAMELIERS *by Oliver Hogue*—A Classic Account of the Australians of the Imperial Camel Corps During the First World War in the Middle East.

RED DUST *by Donald Black*—A Classic Account of Australian Light Horsemen in Palestine During the First World War.

THE LEAN, BROWN MEN *by Angus Buchanan*—Experiences in East Africa During the Great War with the 25th Royal Fusiliers—the Legion of Frontiersmen.

THE NIGERIAN REGIMENT IN EAST AFRICA *by W. D. Downes*—On Campaign During the Great War 1916-1918.

THE 'DIE-HARDS' IN SIBERIA *by John Ward*—With the Middlesex Regiment Against the Bolsheviks 1918-19.

AVAILABLE ONLINE AT **www.leonaur.com**
AND FROM ALL GOOD BOOK STORES

ALSO FROM LEONAUR
AVAILABLE IN SOFTCOVER OR HARDCOVER WITH DUST JACKET

FARAWAY CAMPAIGN by F. James—Experiences of an Indian Army Cavalry Officer in Persia & Russia During the Great War.

REVOLT IN THE DESERT by T. E. Lawrence—An account of the experiences of one remarkable British officer's war from his own perspective.

MACHINE-GUN SQUADRON by A. M. G.—The 20th Machine Gunners from British Yeomanry Regiments in the Middle East Campaign of the First World War.

A GUNNER'S CRUSADE by Antony Bluett—The Campaign in the Desert, Palestine & Syria as Experienced by the Honourable Artillery Company During the Great War.

DESPATCH RIDER by W. H. L. Watson—The Experiences of a British Army Motorcycle Despatch Rider During the Opening Battles of the Great War in Europe.

TIGERS ALONG THE TIGRIS by E. J. Thompson—The Leicestershire Regiment in Mesopotamia During the First World War.

HEARTS & DRAGONS by Charles R. M. F. Crutwell—The 4th Royal Berkshire Regiment in France and Italy During the Great War, 1914-1918.

INFANTRY BRIGADE: 1914 by John Ward—The Diary of a Commander of the 15th Infantry Brigade, 5th Division, British Army, During the Retreat from Mons.

DOING OUR 'BIT' by Ian Hay—Two Classic Accounts of the Men of Kitchener's 'New Army' During the Great War including *The First 100,000* & *All In It*.

AN EYE IN THE STORM by Arthur Ruhl—An American War Correspondent's Experiences of the First World War from the Western Front to Gallipoli-and Beyond.

STAND & FALL by Joe Cassells—With the Middlesex Regiment Against the Bolsheviks 1918-19.

RIFLEMAN MACGILL'S WAR by Patrick MacGill—A Soldier of the London Irish During the Great War in Europe including *The Amateur Army*, *The Red Horizon* & *The Great Push*.

WITH THE GUNS by C. A. Rose & Hugh Dalton—Two First Hand Accounts of British Gunners at War in Europe During World War 1- Three Years in France with the Guns and With the British Guns in Italy.

THE BUSH WAR DOCTOR by Robert V. Dolbey—The Experiences of a British Army Doctor During the East African Campaign of the First World War.

AVAILABLE ONLINE AT **www.leonaur.com**
AND FROM ALL GOOD BOOK STORES

ALSO FROM LEONAUR
AVAILABLE IN SOFTCOVER OR HARDCOVER WITH DUST JACKET

THE 9TH—THE KING'S (LIVERPOOL REGIMENT) IN THE GREAT WAR 1914 - 1918 by Enos H. G. Roberts—Mersey to mud—war and Liverpool men.

THE GAMBARDIER by Mark Severn—The experiences of a battery of Heavy artillery on the Western Front during the First World War.

FROM MESSINES TO THIRD YPRES by Thomas Floyd—A personal account of the First World War on the Western front by a 2/5th Lancashire Fusilier.

THE IRISH GUARDS IN THE GREAT WAR - VOLUME 1 by Rudyard Kipling—Edited and Compiled from Their Diaries and Papers—The First Battalion.

THE IRISH GUARDS IN THE GREAT WAR - VOLUME 1 by Rudyard Kipling—Edited and Compiled from Their Diaries and Papers—The Second Battalion.

ARMOURED CARS IN EDEN by K. Roosevelt—An American President's son serving in Rolls Royce armoured cars with the British in Mesopatamia & with the American Artillery in France during the First World War.

CHASSEUR OF 1914 by Marcel Dupont—Experiences of the twilight of the French Light Cavalry by a young officer during the early battles of the great war in Europe.

TROOP HORSE & TRENCH by R.A. Lloyd—The experiences of a British Lifeguardsman of the household cavalry fighting on the western front during the First World War 1914-18.

THE EAST AFRICAN MOUNTED RIFLES by C.J. Wilson—Experiences of the campaign in the East African bush during the First World War.

THE LONG PATROL by George Berrie—A Novel of Light Horsemen from Gallipoli to the Palestine campaign of the First World War.

THE FIGHTING CAMELIERS by Frank Reid—The exploits of the Imperial Camel Corps in the desert and Palestine campaigns of the First World War.

STEEL CHARIOTS IN THE DESERT by S. C. Rolls—The first world war experiences of a Rolls Royce armoured car driver with the Duke of Westminster in Libya and in Arabia with T.E. Lawrence.

WITH THE IMPERIAL CAMEL CORPS IN THE GREAT WAR by Geoffrey Inchbald—The story of a serving officer with the British 2nd battalion against the Senussi and during the Palestine campaign.

AVAILABLE ONLINE AT **www.leonaur.com**
AND FROM ALL GOOD BOOK STORES

Lightning Source UK Ltd.
Milton Keynes UK
UKHW011205211019
352003UK00001B/111/P